intelligent inquirer, and then, in detail, distinguishes between fact, fiction, and faith. He answers each question thoughtfully and frankly, avoiding technical terms whenever possible and at the same time avoiding the glib, popularized concepts found in over-simplified studies. Professor Martin offers no easy or dogmatic answers, but through these discussions the reader is given an illuminating view of the development of Christian history and the growth of theology during the first two or three centuries.

Fact, Fiction, and Faith is the book to turn to for further insight into Christianity. It was not written primarily for theologians or religious experts, but rather for the thoughtful reader and young student who seek explicit clarification before making a mature judgment on the merits of the Christian faith.

JAMES ALFRED MARTIN, Jr., former Crosby Professor of Religion, Amherst College, is the recently appointed Danforth Professor of Religion in Higher Education, Union Theological Seminary. An Ordained Deacon of the Protestant Episcopal Church, he served as a USNR Chaplain in the Pacific Theater, 1944-46. Professor Martin is the author of *Empirical Philosophies of Religion* and co-author of *Ways of Faith*.

FACT, FICTION, & FAITH

By JAMES ALFRED MARTIN, Jr.

. .
.

NEW YORK

OXFORD UNIVERSITY PRESS

1960

To Ann

© 1960 Oxford University Press, Inc.

Library of Congress Catalogue Card Number: 61–5478

Printed in the United States of America

Preface

Is Christianity obsolete? Many thoughtful people today are convinced that it is. Some of them have been brought up in the faith, but they find that it no longer makes much sense, and that it seems to have little relevance to their lives or the life of the modern world. Others have known the faith only from the outside, but what they have known about it makes it difficult for them to see how intelligent people can take it seriously. Both groups have many honest questions and doubts about Christianity. Yet it seems that many spokesmen for Christianity do not hear or understand the questions, and do not fully respect the doubts. When they address a word to the perplexed, what they say only increases the perplexity.

This book attempts to formulate as accurately and straightforwardly as possible some of the questions and doubts most frequently expressed by those who can make little sense of Christianity as they understand it, but who would like to understand it better. Each question or comment is followed by a brief statement designed to distinguish between fact, fiction, and faith in those aspects of Christianity to which the questions and doubts call attention. The aim is not to convert, but to clarify. Some readers may find their doubts confirmed by the answers herein presented. Others may find that their questions spring more from misunderstanding than from disagreement with the faith in its historic essentials.

The book is not written primarily for theological experts or religious professionals. Yet the author does not want to insult the intelligence of readers who want thoughtful answers and are willing to think in order to get them. He does not claim to be an expert in many of the areas with which a book of this scope must deal. But he has given considerable attention to the questions here presented, in college classrooms and elsewhere. It is his hope that the clarifications attempted may enable the reader to make more intelligent and mature judgments about the Christian faith.

The author is grateful to all who have raised the questions with him, and to all who have aided him in arriving at some answers. Some readers will discern the special influence of many to whom he is particularly indebted in his interpretation of Christianity.

J. A. M. JR.

July 1960

Contents

simple Christian faith into a theological puzzle. . . . How could God, if he existed, be a man? Or why should the experience of one man be any more significant for the understanding of God than the experience of other men? . . . What in the world does it mean to say that God is both three and one? What's all this talk about a Father and a Son and a Holy Ghost, and yet only one God?"

58

IV

"Christians haven't been satisfied with that—they have added dogma to dogma in long and complicated creeds which people are required to believe. . . . Instead of concentrating on living in the spirit of Jesus, Christians have gotten all involved in the paraphernalia of worship and church organization. . . . All this Christian doctrine sounds nice, but is it logical? It all assumes the existence of God—but can you *prove* the existence of God?"

90

V

"Of course when Christians are pressed on any of these matters they always say it's a 'matter of faith.' What is that? How can an honest person say he believes something that can't be proved, or that he knows isn't so? . . . (Augustine: a case-study in faith and reason). . . . How could you square the existence of a good God with the existence of so much suffering and evil in the world?"

126

VI

"Surely it won't do to say that it will all work out in an after-life, because immortality can't be proved either. . . . What would be the point of human effort if everything were in the hands of God anyway? . . . Christianity might make some sense as a private philosophy of life. . . . But who could ever think he had life all figured out?"

160

FACT, FICTION, & FAITH

I

"Christianity may be of sentimental or historical interest . . . but it hardly seems relevant to life in a scientific age. . . . After all, it came from a situation radically different from our own . . . and we have relatively meager information about its origins. . . . People had better use their reason to understand as much of life as they can, and develop their own resources for taking the hard knocks, rather than rely on a crutch like religion. . . . There are some good things in life which should be cherished for their own sake. . . and plenty of worthwhile social and political causes to serve. . . . Religion has bred too much hypocrisy and escapism."

"Christianity may be of sentimental or historical interest . . ."

Many readers of this book may be interested in the Christian faith primarily on sentimental grounds. Reared in Christian families, subjected to some instruction in the faith at an early age, and even waxing mawkish on occasion about the virtues of parents or grandparents for whom the faith was the basis of life, they frequently wonder what the faith is actually all about. They remember a few Bible stories, some Sunday School classes, and some uncomfortable hours spent in church. They probably consider themselves Christian—in the broad sense of the term—and when life becomes particularly trying they may even try a prayer or two, go to church again, and make a firm resolve to bring their religious education up to date. But the pressures and comforts of the daily routine soon put an end to that, and the old family Bible goes back on the shelf. In a vague way it's nice to

3

know that it is there, but there is a lurking suspicion that it won't bear too much looking into. Perhaps it is better to leave religion alone, except on patriotic occasions, or for weddings and funerals, or at Easter and Christmas. After all, many pleasant memories are associated with the latter, and probably the youngsters should get in on them too.

Other readers will agree that some historical knowledge of the faith is good, not only for the youngsters but for any educated person, because, after all, our culture is based in part on a Judeo-Christian heritage. Whatever one may think of Christianity now, they would say, one must recognize the tremendous role it has played in the history of Western civilization. Many of our moral ideals, and much of our finest art, took shape under the aegis of the Christian tradition. If one is to treasure and appreciate much of what is most prized in our culture, it is probably a good idea to know something about the men and events of the Christian past. Indeed, one might even say that before the scientific revolution it probably made sense for the best minds of our culture to find meaning in a Christian world-view—it was all they knew. But the Soviet Union may not be far wrong in turning most churches into museums, while still keeping a few open for those who find need for that sort of thing. One can appreciate the historical values of the past without trying to live in it! (Not that such an attitude is Communistic, of course—one can also take this view in the interest of enlightened democracy.)

". . . but it hardly seems relevant to life in a scientific age."

Many of the questions men once answered in theological terms are now much better answered by science. All sorts of things which people were once willing to attribute simply to the mysterious "will of God" we can now understand in terms of the normal operations of nature. First God became an unnecessary hypothesis for understanding the physical universe, and then Darwin showed that the evolution of all living things can be perfectly well understood without invoking a creator. More recently, psychologists and social scientists have been explaining more and more facts of human life which people formerly talked about in terms of "soul" and "divine law." It is felt that one just doesn't need religion, Christian or other, to understand the world—indeed, he would be better off to forget the quaint pre-scientific views of Christianity, except for the historical and sentimental values they may have. One must be careful, however, not to let sentiment qualify one's full acceptance of the accomplishments and promise of science.

Furthermore, we are now much more aware of other religions and other codes of morality than our forefathers were. The science of anthropology has showed us that different cultures have different religions, and that men can be happy under a wide variety of systems of belief. We "happen" to believe some of the things we do, it is said, simply because our culture "happens" to have developed that way. And even within our own culture we know many happy, moral people who seem to have no need for the faith of their fathers, or any other faith. Thus it is indeed difficult for many to see why the Christian faith *can* be of more than sentimental or historical interest now.

"After all, it came from a situation radically different from our own . . ."

5

The situation in Biblical times was different in many respects. Not only was there little or no science to explain things, but the world in which most people lived was much simpler and tidier. At least, so it seems at first glance. But then if one begins to examine in some detail the Roman world of the first century, one may have to admit that many of the fundamental problems we face today were problems for men then, too. On the surface there was peace, progress, and prosperity. Rome had picked up the pieces of the Hellenistic world that Alexander the Great had put together in an amazing political structure. Roman legions and Roman law had brought the *Pax Romana* to much of the civilized world of the West, and to parts of the East. Roman roads and the widespread knowledge of the Latin and Greek languages made communication between parts of the empire possible in a way which has scarcely been equaled since. But since so many peoples and cultures were brought together in the empire, there was bound to be some tension, and many people became confused and they hankered after "the good old days" of a simpler life. Some of them continued to turn to the old superstitions of the magical and polytheistic religions, just as some people today turn to the religion of our past for similar reasons. But the better-educated and ruling classes were beginning to turn to a more rational view of things, and there were many philosophies from which they could choose to find meaning for their lives. It may be said that the Roman world of the first century was one world, looking for one faith. It is not surprising that many people thought they had found that faith when Christianity emerged from Palestine.

". . . and we have relatively meager information about its origins."

Most of the information we have about the origins of Christianity is found in the pages of the New Testament, and the New Testament is the official literature of the Christian church. There are scattered references to the faith in the works of the Jewish historian Josephus, and notices of it in Roman historians from the time when Christians had become sufficiently numerous and obnoxious to be persecuted. But most of our information is Biblical—and the entire New Testament contains fewer words than a Sunday edition of *The New York Times*. The information is therefore indeed meager, in terms of documents and words, and much of it could be classed as propaganda: its intent is primarily to propagate the faith.

Yet it is not surprising that this is the case. After all, Palestine was in a relatively obscure province of the Roman empire. It was, and is today, of great strategic importance, since it is part of the land-bridge between Africa, Asia, and Europe. But it was relatively poor economically, and its inhabitants, the Jews, seemed to be a strange and troublesome people. They seemed to take their religion too seriously. A century before, they had fought a war for independence on religious grounds, and they had won, against great odds. But they had not been able to maintain their independence; the Romans had been invited in to keep peace. Even so, the Jews were not happy. They resented even the relatively benign Roman rule, and they were involved in religious quarrels among themselves. They had the curious idea that there was only one God; and they had the affrontery to claim that this God had uniquely revealed his will through their turbulent history—that they were a "Chosen People," chosen to enlighten the entire world religiously! No wonder the Romans would have little interest in the life and execution of a wandering Jewish rabbi—carpenter by trade—who was said to claim to be King of the Jews. And when people began to show up in Rome who claimed that this rabbi was either a god or a demi-god, their message could barely be tolerated as just another of those superstitions about dying and rising savior-gods coming out of the East in the form of so-called "mystery religions." It is not surprising that our information about the origins of Christianity is so meager. It is surprising that we have as much from the first century as we have.

Of what does this information consist? The fact that the Christians called their collection of first-century literature The New Testament indicates that they thought of it as being continuous with, but somehow fulfilling, the literature and history of the Jews. The idea of a testament, or covenant—as in "last will and testament"—had been a central idea in the Jewish faith. The Lord Jehovah, the Jews believed, had entered into a covenant with them. He had called their father, Abraham, out of Ur in the lower Mesopotamian basin and into Palestine, which he gave them as their land. His special concern for the Jews had been demonstrated in many events recalled in the stories of the Old Testament patriarchs. Pre-eminent among these events was the deliverance of the people out of bondage in Egypt, through the work of Moses. After the exodus the Lord had formalized the covenant, reminding the people of Israel of the unmerited favor, or grace, he had showed them, and binding them to him through divinely revealed law. They were to be his people, and he would be their God. They were chosen, not so much for special privilege as for special responsibility—to obey and to teach the commandments of God among all people, until all people enjoyed a universal peace based on moral law. In their subsequent history the Jews were told many times that they had failed their trust. Prophets were sent to warn them of the consequences of personal and national infidelity, and their history was turbulent indeed. But through it all they clung to the idea of covenant, and to the conviction that sooner or later God would accomplish his righteous purposes for mankind.

Many believed that these purposes would be accomplished through a special agent of God called *Messiah*, "the anointed one." As kings and prophets had been anointed in the past to carry out the divine will in history, so at the climactic fulfillment of history there would come a special "anointed one." Some thought he would be a Son of David, a political savior recalling and restoring the Golden Age of Israel's past. Some looked for a Son of Man, a quasi-divine being coming on clouds of glory in the midst of a great historical cataclysm, to set up a New Age in a New Earth. Christians believed that the Messiah had come, in the person and work of Jesus of Nazareth. This was the "good news" (gospel) which they proclaimed, first to their Jewish compatriots, and then throughout the Roman world. Their message seemed as offensive to the Jews as it seemed foolish to the Gentiles. But increasing numbers accepted it as the "gospel truth"—the true good news about life and its meaning—containing divine power for triumphant living.

These were the people who found it necessary, less than a generation after Jesus' death, to write down the traditions about him which had circulated by word of

9

mouth among the small Christian communities in the first few years of the Christian movement. As long as itinerant eye-witnesses were around and the community small, there was no need for much writing. Writing was a more esoteric and specialized craft then than it is now, and the Jews had developed a remarkable talent for accurate oral transmission of tradition, as current archaeological and literary research into their later, written, tradition is constantly proving. But in A.D. 70 there was a final, abortive, uprising of the Jews against Rome. Jerusalem was destroyed, and most of the Jews, Christian and non-Christian, were dispersed throughout the Roman world. Written communication and preservation of tradition became imperative if the Jewish or Christian ways of life were to survive. It was about A.D. 70 that the first of the "gospels," the Gospel according to St. Mark, was written.

Prior to that time, however, Christian documents had been in circulation among the churches of the Eastern Mediterranean basin. The Apostle Paul had written numerous letters to churches he had founded, giving them practical advice on problems of faith and morals which had arisen among them. He had also written a more formal theological introduction to himself for the church in Rome, which he hoped to visit, and did finally visit in chains. As similar points of doctrine and conduct were debated in various churches, Paul's letters were circulated among them, to be read at Christian worship services. Thus were the earliest parts of the New Testament written and preserved—the first of them dating about A.D. 50, or less than two decades after Jesus' execution.

In Paul's letters there is little mention of the details of the life of Jesus; he seems to assume knowledge of this among his readers. It is the significance of the life that Paul is most eager to communicate; and for him the significance came to a focus in the crucifixion and the resurrection. The gospels also give relatively more information about the last week of Jesus' life than about the rest of it. They were not intended by their authors to be biographies, in the modern sense of the term. Rather they were meant to be versions of the gospel, the good news, and each version bears the imprint of the good-news spreader ("evangelist") who wrote it. Since most of the information contained in Mark's gospel is also found in Matthew and Luke, and since the latter follow the general chronological framework of Mark, it is generally assumed that Mark's was written first. The picture of Jesus given by Mark is that of a man in a hurry. No information about his birth or early life is included. The story begins with the beginning of Jesus' public ministry at his baptism, and moves swiftly through early popularity to rising opposition and the climax of the crucifixion. The emphasis is more upon powerful deeds than upon formal teaching.

Matthew and Luke seem to come from a period about two decades later than Mark. Matthew follows a scheme of alternating teaching with narrative, and he seems to be primarily interested in showing the relation of Jesus to his Jewish background, and of Christianity to Judaism. Luke, the physician-companion of Paul, is a more polished writer. In the prologue to his gospel, dedicated to one Theophilus, he indicates that many had attempted to do what he is doing, having derived their information, as did he, from eye-witnesses. He assumes some familiarity with the traditions on the part of his reader. But he wishes to give a more orderly account than others have given, and to show, in a two-volume work—Luke and the Acts of the Apostles—how Christianity originated in Palestine and eventually found its way to Rome. He finds it necessary to explain some Jewish customs and ideas to his Gentile audience as he goes along, showing at times an inaccurate understanding of some of them!

The fourth gospel, attributed to St. John, differs in style and form from the other three. Since the others agree on fundamental chronology and contain much common material, they are called the synoptic gospels, giving a common synopsis or viewing-together of the life of Jesus. The fourth gospel opens with a poetic, theological prologue in which the basic themes of the writer's interpretation of Jesus are set forth. The narrative which follows is interwoven with interpretive material, sometimes in the form of discourses of Jesus. The chronology differs from that of the synoptics in that the public ministry of Jesus is depicted as beginning in Judea rather than in Galilee, and as extending over three years rather than twelve to eighteen months. The general tenor of the work suggests a period of time a decade or more later than that of the synoptics, though recent scholarship in the Dead Sea Scrolls and other documents seems to indicate an authenticity in the fourth gospel's portrayal of first-century Judaism which was previously unappreciated. Some of its narrative portions may be of earlier oral origin than those of the synoptics.

Other letters of early Christian leaders make up the rest of the New Testament, and the last book included is a tract for churches undergoing persecution, calling them to more faithful witness by means of a magnificently symbolic vision of the divine fulfillment of history. Thus, in some respects "our knowledge of the origins of Christianity is meager" indeed. But in others it is surprisingly rich; and to the trained scholar, using the tools of modern literary and historical criticism, it reveals a tremendous amount of information about the nature of the Christian faith and the life of the Christian community in the first, exciting century of its existence.

"People had better use their reason to understand as much of life as they can, and develop their own resources for taking the hard knocks, rather than rely on a crutch like religion."

There were many people in the world into which Christianity came who held precisely this view. The most prominent school of thought to which they gave allegiance was that of the Stoics. The school derived its name from the fact that its founder, Zeno, taught from a *stoa*—a porch or arcade—in Athens. And the philosophy he taught was a front-porch or marketplace philosophy: he counseled men to face life squarely in all its complexity, and to be masters of their own souls. His view, like that of some moderns who turn to Stoicism as a philosophy of life, frequently without knowing its classical formulations, was born of disillusionment. A predecessor, Antisthenes, had decided that there is nothing in life you can count on not to let you down except yourself. Pleasures are fleeting, and most of the causes to which men give themselves turn out to be self-defeating. "Let me be mad rather than experience pleasure!" Antisthenes is alleged to have said. Rather, let men cultivate the virtues of courage and self-sufficiency—the virtues so well displayed by man's best friend, the dog. The *can*-ic (or canine) life is the good life, he said . . . and his followers were called "*can*-ics" or "cynics." One of them, the celebrated Diogenes, went around Athens in daylight with a lighted lamp "looking for a man"—and never finding a *true* man, he said. In other words, beatniks are not new to the world.

Zeno and the Stoics, however, had a somewhat broader view of things. They did trust human reason, up to a point. And, unlike some of their modern followers, they asked what must be true of the world if reason is to be trusted. How does one account for the fact that much of the world *can* be understood, and that actions based on rational reflection are more likely to work out than those which are not? Zeno was impressed by the regularities of nature, which astronomers of his day were tracing in new and exciting ways in the world beyond the earth—in the cosmos itself. The fact that man can understand this order by expressing it in an orderly system of language, and that he can predict some events of nature on the basis of his knowledge, was for Zeno the most astounding fact of life. It seemed to suggest that there is a sort of divine order or "Reason" (*Logos*) at the heart of things, and that in each man there is a spark of this divine reason. In other words, Zeno's rationalism became a kind of religion. Perhaps modern rationalists do not realize that theirs may, too; or perhaps they don't go on to ask the more ultimate questions which Zeno asked about the miracle of reason and a rational universe. In any event, on the basis of his religious rationalism Zeno could go on to speak of the equality, or "brotherhood," of men based on the fact that all men are rational, and thus sons of a common divine "Father."

Of course the Stoics did not believe that life always works out just the way reasonable men think it should. There is ignorance in the world, and there are conflicts of will between men and nations. But the good man can determine how he will react to the events he experiences.

He can enjoy the good and learn to be indifferent to the evil—or conquer it when he can. It is never enough for the good man to "do the best he can *under* the circumstances"; insofar as he can, he should strive to be *on top of* the circumstances. And when circumstances are too much for one, one always has the final freedom to ask, "To be, or not to be?" and to choose not to be rather than to be under some circumstances. There is always available to the Stoic the last sacrament of suicide.

The Stoic way, in one form or another, has always commended itself to many thoughtful people; it did in Jesus' day, and it does in ours. But some who accept it, as well as some who do not, see in it a final sadness. Robert Frost, in his *Masque of Mercy*, has one of his characters say "The saddest thing in life is that the best thing in it should be courage." Why should men feel this sadness? Would some other view of the world sound like good news? It did in the first century—perhaps it may still. In any event, it is important to note that Stoicism is also a *faith*, insofar as it *assumes* certain things to be true about life and counsels men to act on those assumptions. In advising men to turn from the "crutches" of other faiths to self-sufficiency, modern Stoics might ask just how sufficient the self is. They might at least realize, as the ancient Stoics did, that the self is not its own creator, and also that "no man is an island unto himself." Men are bound together in mutual dependencies, on each other and on "Nature," if not on God. Dependency means responsibility. Is it enough to say that one is responsible, finally, only to oneself—"this above all, to thine own self be true"? And, finally, is it true that the final reach of man's freedom is his freedom to commit suicide? Many people asked these questions of Stoicism in the world into which Christianity came.

"There are some good things in life which should be cherished for their own sake . . ."

Again, many people in the world into which Christianity came would agree. In Antisthenes' day there were those who took a tack directly opposite his and held that pleasure is the only thing one can be sure of. They were called Cyrenaics. The aim of all philosophies and religions is allegedly to bring men happiness or pleasure, they said; so why not go directly to the point and take one's pleasures when and where one can find them? Life is too uncertain to permit too much deliberation about ways and means to pleasure. Is it not better to "seize the day"—to eat, drink, and be merry when and while one can? The Cyrenaics would have revised A. E. Housman's little couplet to affirm that "Malt does more than Milton can / To justify God's ways to man." The way of the Cyrenaics continues to appeal to many people, including many who have never thought through the implications of their faith in pleasure, or have never stated its rationale as baldly as did the Cyrenaics.

Others saw, and continue to see, in the Cyrenaic view a crude version of a faith which, in a more sophisticated form, may offer man's best hope for making a good thing of the bad situation in which he finds himself. The more sophisticated version is called Epicureanism, for its classic exponent, Epicurus. Epicurus agreed with the Cyrenaics that pleasure or happiness is the best thing in life. But he saw that the simple eat, drink, and be merry philosophy would not work. While one can live only one day at a time, the probability is that for most of us more

16

days will be ahead. Indiscretion in eating and drinking today—or tonight—may bring pain tomorrow which negates that pleasure. So Epicurus counseled men to choose their pleasures wisely, and to indulge in them sanely and in moderation. Indeed, he went on to point out that the pleasures of the flesh are not really the most intense or the most abiding pleasures men can know. There are the deeper and more lasting joys of friendship, of art, and of good conversation. So he set up his school, appropriately, in a quiet garden. It will not do for men to get too much involved in the affairs of society, as the Stoics were urging them to do, he said. One must withdraw from the ways of the madding crowd and cultivate the simple but profound pleasures of the garden. Epicurus' most influential Roman exponent, Lucretius, who in his poem *On the Nature of Things* hailed Epicurus as a savior, speaks of the pleasure of looking out on the confused world from the refuge of one's enlightened position—like one safe on shore looking out on storm-tossed sailors at sea. Lucretius did not mean that one should derive pleasure from the misfortunes or ignorance of others. But his statement does suggest a question which many thoughtful people have asked about his faith: Is salvation only for intellectuals? Can only those "in the know" enjoy life, and is their number destined always to be small? When Christians appeared in the Roman world proclaiming meaning and happiness in life for all sorts and conditions of men—not excluding intellectuals—many heard them as bearers of news which was good indeed.

One thing that attracted many to Christianity was that it seemed to have good news about death as well as about life. And this is also what attracted men like Lucretius to Epicureanism. Not only must men have freedom from want, by keeping their physical needs at a minimum, said Lucretius; they must also have freedom from fear. There is always a fearful overtone in the simple eat, drink, and be merry slogan, ". . . for tomorrow we die." It is the fear of death which is the chief corrupter of man's pleasure, Lucretius said. Epicurus brought the good news that men have no reason to fear death. From the fear of death, and fancies about an after-life, they have generated also fear of the gods, who are supposed to inflict terrible punishments on those who, consciously or otherwise, have transgressed their decrees. And from the control of gods over the after-life it is a short step to belief in the control of gods over this life, with all its attendant priestcraft and superstition. Fear of death and fear of the gods are the two chief fears from which men must be saved if they are to be happy. The good news, said Lucretius and Epicurus, is that a way has been found in science, and a scientific view of the world. The science to which they referred was that of Democritus, who had attempted to show that everything in the world can be understood in terms of atoms swirling in the void.

All that is, is composed of material which may be broken down to least-divisible or "un-cuttable" (*a-tomic*) units, said Democritus. From all eternity these atoms fall through the void, colliding with each other and forming new units of varying shapes and sizes. The earth and all that therein is may be understood in terms of this simple but far-reaching principle. Even that which men call mind or soul is simply a complex arrangement of unusually fine atoms. No god, creator or sustainer, is needed to explain the world. And when men die, the arrangement of atoms which formerly constituted their identity simply passes on into some other arrangement.

They are no more; it is as simple as that. Men get themselves into all sorts of difficulties by trying to imagine what it will be like to be dead. Well, when one is dead, one simply *is not*. Where death is, one is not. Death, in other words, is literally *nothing*. To try to imagine how one will be after he is dead is as stupid as trying to imagine how one was before he was born. Death is nothing—and who should be afraid of nothing? Indeed, death should be welcomed as providing an appropriate end to a happy life. To live indefinitely would be boring indeed. One should graciously make his exit from the stage in order to make room for others. Or, if one's life has been unhappy, then death brings welcome release. In no case is death to be feared, any more than gods are to be feared. If there are gods, they are said to be blessed—and surely this means that they cannot be concerned with the unhappy affairs of men! Rather, they are poetic examples of the tranquility to which men may aspire through the use of their reason and the cultivation of the right kinds of pleasure. Religion, in other words, may have a certain aesthetic or moral *inspirational* value for the enlightened man; but he must be careful not to take the gods literally or too seriously.

The Epicurean view, like the Stoic, continues to attract many thoughtful people in today's world, as it did in the first century. Is there a final sadness about it, too? Does it also take certain things for granted, without pushing too far into the whys and wherefores of them—such as the atoms—void formula for "understanding"? Can it be a faith for all men? Is blessedness, or the most profound happiness men can know, in part dependent on withdrawal from life? Many people were asking these questions in the first century when they heard of a teacher who said: "Blessed—supremely happy—are the pure in heart . . . those who are aware of their spiritual poverty . . . the peacemakers . . . those who are persecuted for righteousness' sake . . . even those who mourn. . ." This teacher, it was said, spoke of a God who was not withdrawn from the tragedy of life, but who participated in it in order to redeem it. The teacher himself, his followers said, had performed a final act of redemption through a tragic death. For some reason men *are* "afraid of nothing" or nothing*ness*. Is death "nothing"? Its "sting" and fear are too well known to the honest man. The Christians said there was better news about death than Lucretius offered.

"*. . . and plenty of worthwhile social and political causes to serve.*"

If one cannot find a sufficient faith for living by turning to his own courage and belief in a rational universe, or to carefully chosen pleasures excluding carefully exorcised—or evaded—fears, then he can always look for meaning in society. Many moderns shift from one of these faiths to the other as circumstances demand—or as becomes necessary when one begins to push any one of them too far, or to ask too many questions about its origin and adequacy. This was true in Jesus' day too. In his day, for many men the symbol of the last bulwark of faith was the Roman eagle—just as in ours it may be the hammer and sickle, or the American flag. Maybe one cannot finally make sense of one's life as a private affair, but surely it makes sense to strive for a better deal for the kids! The better deal may be envisioned as coming through better business, or better labor, or better education. Or it may be envisioned as coming through the strengthening of a political system. Usually it is thought of vaguely as a compound of these. In Jesus' day the Roman eagle was a very concrete symbol of a very definite hope. After all, it was through the genius of the Roman state and the power of Roman arms that much of the world enjoyed a peace and prosperity it had never known before. Was it not, after all, from the state itself that all blessings flowed? Were not the immediate sources of comfort and meaning the political and economic structures of the empire? It is no wonder that Julius Caesar was hailed as *divus Julius* upon his return from the Eastern wars, and that a cult was established in his honor on his death. Augustus Caesar had even more obviously brought good things to the East, and Eastern peoples were accustomed to hailing their rulers as gods. When citizens of the empire burned their pinch of incense to Caesar, therefore, they were doing a perfectly natural thing—as natural as saluting the flag. But for many of them it was also the supreme act of religious devotion, because Caesar symbolized that which they held to be most worthy of man's devotion—the state. The state and the causes it embodies continue to appeal to men as an always-present "other faith," alongside or incorporating the more explicit philosophical or religious faiths with which they may formally identify themselves.

But is the state—local or world—sufficient as an end of devotion? Some people asked this in Jesus' day; many ask it now. A disillusioned Communist has called it *The God That Failed*. For him, Arthur Koestler, the alternative seemed for a while to be *The Yogi or the Commissar*. If political gods fail, then mystic withdrawal is the only way. Not many people in Jesus' day or in ours would hold that the alternatives are so starkly posed. Yet many do vacillate from one to the other, as disturbing questions are asked about "*why* a better deal for the kids?"—or even "why the *kids*?". As favorite causes founder, escape from causes seems to be indicated—or at least the cautious skepticism about them which seems to characterize much of the present younger generation. Men, it is felt, expect either too much or too little from the state. In any case, the state and its causes seem inadequate as a total basis for living, no matter how broadly the concept of the state may be extended or its causes spelled out in terms of social values.

People in the Roman empire who had begun to think thoughts like these were naturally interested in the word of a teacher who had spoken of things that are Caesar's and things that are not. The superpatriots among them could not tolerate the refusal of the teacher's followers to burn the pinch of incense to Caesar, particularly in times of danger for the state. Many of the Christians were executed as traitors. Indeed, the formal charge against the teacher himself, which resulted in his execution, was that he claimed a kingship he did not possess. It was very difficult for many to understand what he and his followers said about a kingdom "not of this world." Loyalty to that kingdom did not seem to conflict entirely with loyalty to the empire; early spokesmen for Christianity were always pointing out that Christians were, on the whole, law-abiding citizens. But, like their Jewish compatriots, they insisted that empires are not embodiments of absolute values—that states and social causes also stand under the judgment of another King. What one was to make of this dual allegiance was as puzzling to non-Christians—and to many Christians—then as it is now.

"Religion has bred too much hypocrisy and escapism."

Perhaps it would be well to pause at this point and ask just what one means by *religion*. As the term is popularly used, it probably means belief in a god or gods, expressed in allegiance to an organized group dedicated to the worship and service of the god or gods. Many would associate the *belief* part with their early instruction in some current system of religion, and the *service* part with obedience to certain moral codes presumably associated with the belief. It is fairly obvious that people do not always practice what they preach, and so some conclude that practice would be improved if the preaching were abandoned. It should be noted that those who hold this view are exhibiting their own allegiance to at least one basic virtue: sincerity. It is better, they say, not to profess to believe things on which one is not willing to act. Such people are themselves committed to certain principles of action, to which they would invite others' commitment. Justice or fair-play; love or mercy; courage or integrity; many words may be offered for the moral values to which those who denounce traditional religion pledge allegiance.

Belief in deity involves not only some sort of intellectual judgment that deity exists, but also a commitment to or trust in deity as the basis and goal of life. Similarly, for those who abandon formal religion there must be judgments that certain ends or values for men are worthwhile, and that the world is such that devotion to those ends is reasonable. In other words, commitments and basic judgments are involved in both cases. And in both cases it is possible for men to act in ways that are not consistent with their announced beliefs. Hypocrisy, in other words, is not uniquely related to organized religion. Indeed, there is an ironic note of hypocrisy in saying, as some critics of churchmen seem to say, "I thank Thee that I am not as those hypocrites who go to church!"

Furthermore, "escapism" is not limited to religion and religious folk. To talk about escapism is to assume some basic judgments as to what "real life" is, in order that it may be contrasted with whatever realm of escape one is denouncing. Usually people in rebellion against traditional religions call them escapist because they think religion directs attention to "other-worldly" values, and promises other-worldly rewards or punishments in such a way as to detract from intelligent effort to achieve such goods as men may enjoy here and now. By promising "pie in the sky when you die," it is said, religion holds up progress in building bigger and better bakeries here and now.

But it may be pointed out that there are many forms of escape from a full engagement with life. Some intellectuals may escape to ivory towers of detached analysis and thereby seek to evade the moral demands of family and community responsibilities. A scientist may use his laboratory as a refuge from sticky problems of life, and a business or professional man may use his office or his practice as a retreat. Some may try to escape into pleasure. A "sense of duty," expressed in busy-ness, may be others' escape from pressing personal problems. In any case, escapism is not indigenous to religious folk only.

Yet the fact remains that, as William Temple, late Archbishop of Canterbury, once remarked, "the Church is probably the most effective device man has yet found to protect himself from God"—or from fully responsible living in terms of rationally chosen values. The word "God" has stood for, among other things, that to which—

or He to Whom—men have felt they owed final allegiance. God is that which—or He Who—is, in the last analysis, believed to be trustworthy. Religions that use the word "God" for the object—or Subject—of final trust have indeed betrayed their announced trust in many ways. But note that it was an Archbishop who made the remark about the Church. In so doing he was standing in the tradition of prophetic criticism which has always constituted part of the heritage of Judaism and Christianity. Someone has said that the only effective reforms of religion have come from within religion. Whether this be true or not, it is true that the Christian tradition has again and again turned to a principle of prophetic protest against sham and hypocrisy in attempts to reform itself.

Notice the phrase "prophetic protest." In the tradition into which Jesus was born there had been a long line of prophets who, at various junctures in Israel's history, had sought to recall Israel to her original trust in and commitment to the covenant-God of the exodus from Egypt and the Law of Sinai. Again and again the people of Israel were tempted to find meaning and security for themselves through allegiance to other gods. When the Hebrew bedouins came into Palestine, a relatively advanced agrarian civilization, it seemed logical for them to worship the fertility-gods of the soil called Baals— "Lords" or "Husbands" to whom their worshippers "belonged." Weather, seasons, and processes of reproduction and fertilization seemed to be the immediate sources of life and meaning. The prophets, from Elijah to Ezekiel, labored mightily to convince the Jews that the historical, redeeming God of Sinai was also Lord of the earth. This Lord, they said, demanded a convenant of brotherhood among men. They perceived that the new civilization of the Jews in Palestine was based on economic structures which bred oppression and injustice. And they saw that men used the paraphernalia of formal religious worship as a way of covering up their infidelity to the God of the covenant. "I hate, I despise your feast days, and I will not listen to the noise of your songs," the prophet Amos portrayed the Lord as saying; rather, "let justice run down like waters, and righteousness as a mighty stream." Isaiah of Jerusalem saw signs of infidelity in Judah's anxious attempts to play the game of power-politics in order to maintain her national security among the great empires of his day. He and others denounced those who would "go to Egypt for horses and chariots," that is, those who would pin their hopes on the latest in armaments.

Jerusalem did finally fall to the Babylonians, and many thought that with the loss of the capital and the land, the temple and the apparatus of formal religious worship, the basis of Israel's faith was lost too. But others continued, in exile, to hold to the prophetic faith in a God who transcends temples and homelands. They saw to it that this faith was taught in synagogues, and that the documents which had proclaimed it were preserved. When the Jews returned from exile they set up a church-state designed to bring all of life under the control of the God of the fathers, and to translate the insights of the prophets into laws. In due time, they believed, the redeemer-God of the covenant would bring his purpose of peace based on justice for all men to fulfillment through the Messiah.

In the time of Jesus most Jews believed that trust in God should be expressed through obedience to his revealed Law, and that such obedience would be rewarded by material well-being for the righteous individual and, eventually, by social redemption for all men through the work of the Messiah. But there were disagreements as to what the Law was. The group called Sadducees accepted only the commandments included in the Books of Moses, the first five books of the Bible. This left them free to devise their own laws for many areas of life not explicitly dealt with in these books—and they were to be found mainly among the wealthy, landowning classes! Furthermore, they believed in no resurrection of the dead, because they did not find this belief taught in the lawbooks—and they were doing very well, here and now, by means which might not bear divine judgment in a resurrection! Another group, the Pharisees, believed that laws must be indefinitely multiplied as the situations of life change and necessitate new applications of old principles. They accepted, therefore, the further elaborations of the lawyers, and strove mightily to obey the letter of the law in their daily lives. One of them said that if all Israel fully obeyed the law for one day God would send the Messiah. A group called Essenes decided that it was impossible to obey the law of God while immersed in the ways of a wicked society; so they withdrew to communal monastic centers like the one at Qmran, whose scriptures constitute part of the Dead Sea Scrolls, there to wait patiently for God to send the Messiah.

All of these groups agreed that the heart of religion lies in doing the will of God, and they all believed that men can both know and do the divine will. Religion thus became primarily a matter of *do's* and *don'ts;* of *thou shalts* and *thou shalt nots.* Acceptance by God, for the individual or for the nation, depended on proving worthiness to be accepted.

II

"Everyone knows that you ought to be good, and Jesus taught
that if you are morally perfect you will enter the Kingdom of
God. . . . Christianity has moved a long way from the simple
ethics of the Sermon on the Mount and the simple courage
and kindness of Jesus. Even in the New Testament these got
all mixed up with the conviction that he was a supernatural
being. What is one to make of the claim that he was born of a
virgin? . . . or that he performed miracles? . . . All this business about Jesus' death being a sacrifice for man's sins just
doesn't make sense. . . . What about the resurrection?."

*"Everyone knows that you ought to be good, and Jesus taught
that if you are morally perfect you will enter the Kingdom
of God."*

In the Sermon on the Mount, and in many other teachings, Jesus called this view radically into question. It is
true, he said, that blessedness, or supreme happiness,
depends on purity of heart and following the way of
the peacemaker. But it also depends on a recognition of
one's moral inadequacy and spiritual poverty: "Blessed
are the poor in spirit . . . the meek." It had been said that
in order to be accepted by God, men must do no murder.
It was relatively easy for most "good" people to avoid
this crime. But anyone who has ever entertained hatred
in his heart for his brother, said Jesus, has willed his
nonexistence to some degree; let the "good" man also

become free of hatred. It had been said that one should not commit adultery; again, most good people could avoid that crime. But any man who has ever looked upon a woman with lust in his heart has desired that relationship which adultery makes explicit; let the good man also be free of lust, said Jesus. In other words, it is not so much *what* men do as *why* they do it that counts in the sight of God. And if they would make themselves *worthy* of acceptance by God, then nothing less than *perfection,* of motive as well as of deed, will do: "Be ye therefore perfect, even as your Father in Heaven is perfect." Of what does the Heavenly Father's perfection consist? Well, he makes the sun to shine and the rain to fall on the just and the unjust alike; he cares with an infinite care for the smallest sparrow, and thus surely also for every human being made in his image. If one would make himself worthy of the divine love, then he must perfectly emulate the divine love. But what man can do this? The commands of the Sermon on the Mount seem to constitute a final judgment on all of man's pretenses to righteousness. If one wants to put his relationship to God, or to life, on a bargaining basis, then the message of the Sermon on the Mount is not good news, but bad news indeed!

But Jesus said that entering into the fullness of life is not a matter of *earning* the right to do so. His term for the fullness of life was Kingdom of God. The keynote of his message, from beginning to end, was "repent, for the Kingdom of God is at hand." By repentance he meant a radical about-face, a radical reversal of the values by which men "naturally" live. To repent is to see oneself as self-centered, striving to be self-sufficient. He never offered an explicit definition of Kingdom of God. Perhaps the closest he came was in the prayer he taught his disciples to pray, the so-called Lord's Prayer. In it, following a recognition of the existence and holiness of God, is the petition "thy kingdom come, thy will be done on earth as it is in heaven." Here the second phrase may be taken as a paraphrase of the first, after the manner of Hebrew parallelism found in the Psalms and elsewhere: "thy kingdom come . . . *which is to say,* thy will be done . . ." The King*dom* of God is wherever his king*ship* is recognized; where his will is done. "Heaven" is the state of perfect conformity to the divine will, and the fulfillment of the divine purpose. "May earth be heaven!" is another way of saying "thy will be done on earth as it is in heaven."

To live in the Kingdom of God, then, is to live life as it was intended to be lived: *really* to live, in harmony with the will of God, or the authentic structure of life. The Kingdom *is* whenever and wherever men are willing so to live. It is a *present* reality to the extent that men accept the conditions for entering it, and embody it in their living. It is a *future* reality as the perfection of life. In Jesus' day Jews spoke of "this age," characterized largely by disobedience to the divine will, with its attendant evils, and "the age to come"—the Messianic age in which the kingship of God would be fully established. It should be noted that the age to come was not thought of as something "out of this world." Rather, it would constitute a "new creation," or a *re*-creation of life in accord with the divine purpose. The good news, said Jesus, is that this Kingdom is "at hand." He saw signs of its presence in the healing of disease, the acceptance of forgiveness by the wicked, and the elevation of the poor. It was at hand—and yet it is also yet to come in its fullness. When that day is to be no man knows, said Jesus. But he seems to have felt increasingly that his life and, finally, his death were uniquely bound up with its coming.

In any event, the Kingdom was "at hand," he said,— now open and available. Men could reach out and touch it, as it were; they could enter it if they would. But how could they? Not, as we have previously noted, by striving to be good enough to enter. The Pharisees, said Jesus, "would take the Kingdom by storm" through their righteousness. They would *force* their acceptance— would force God to send the Kingdom, by being good. The Pharisees seemed to think that goodness provides a way of manipulating God. By putting a sufficient amount of goodness in the slot, as it were, one may force the divine machinery to produce a proportionate amount of happiness, now or later. But men who so believe, said Jesus, have never really asked what degree or quality of goodness could be enough to warrant entrance into the Kingdom. If it is the perfection demanded in the Sermon on the Mount, what man can enter the Kingdom? "Fear not, little flock," said Jesus, "it is your Father's good pleasure to *give* you the Kingdom"! That which men cannot earn is available to them as a divine gift, if they will accept it on the terms of the giver. The Lord of the Kingdom is not a strict balancer-of-accounts; he is the loving father who wills the good of his children. The only requirement for entrance into the joy of the Kingdom is recognition of one's spiritual poverty and a willingness to be forgiven.

Jesus made this point in story after story. It should be noted that he did not teach in formal discourses, or according to fixed pedagogical formulas. The Sermon on the Mount is itself probably a collection of statements made by Jesus on various occasions, put together for teaching purposes by the early Christian community. His teaching was more spontaneous and *ad lib,* addressed on the spur of the moment to the needs of specific occasions. He taught on the seashore, in the marketplace, in the fields, on the hillsides of Galilee. His favorite teaching device was the parable, a simple story using an event of everyday life to make a point about the nature of God and man's relation to him; to make a point, in other words, about *authentic* life. Jesus used all sorts of people and events in his parables. Some of them are admirable, some scandalous. In each case his intent was to make a point about God and his relation to man—not to counsel men to imitate all the characters of the parable in all respects.

Thus, with respect to conditions for entrance into the Kingdom, Jesus once told a story of man who needed day-laborers to help gather in his harvest. Early in the morning he went to the local employment office, the marketplace, and hired a number of men for an agreed wage, "a penny a day" (purchasing power apparently equivalent to the normal day's wage). Later in the day he realized that more men would be needed, so he returned to the marketplace and hired more, on the same agreement. Finally, late in the day he returned once again to get a few more men to finish up the day's work. "Why have you been here idle all day?" he asked. "Because no man hired us," they said. They were willing and open to work, but they had not been called. "Come along, then," said the employer, "and whatever is right I'll give you." And the men came—not after collective bargaining as the others had come, but freely trusting in the good faith of the employer. At the end of the day the employer instructed his paymaster to pay off—beginning with those last hired. They each received a penny. Then those hired earlier were paid—and they also received a penny! At that they were fit to be tied. A spokesman cried out, "Unjust!" Those who had worked all day on a bargaining basis received the same as those who came late, asking no questions. "Is your heart evil because mine is good?" the employer asked. "Have I not the right to accept and reward those whom I will, on my own terms?" Should those who believe only in justice begrudge the mercy of the merciful one? The "point" about the nature of God, and of the conditions for entrance into the "vineyard" of the Kingdom should be clear.

The same point is made in one of Jesus' most famous stories, the so-called Parable of the Prodigal Son. A rich man had two sons. One day the younger demanded his inheritance, which his father gave him. The son forthwith went off to "waste his substance in riotous living." When it was all gone he came to one fine morning in a pig-pen. He would be infinitely better off, he thought, if he were the poorest day-laborer on his father's farm. So, in honest recognition of what he had done with his freedom and his freely given wealth, he swallowed his pride—which is a larger mouthful than most men can manage—and headed home. But when he "was yet a long way off" his father saw him and, instead of waiting for him to come to make amends, rushed out to meet him and "fell upon his neck and kissed him." The son was overcome. He felt that he still had to get out his confession and make his repentance—his "coming to himself"—known. But the father immediately gave orders that preparations should be made for a homecoming banquet. The fatted calf was to be killed, and everyone was to eat, drink, and be merry, because he who was lost was found; he who had strayed from home had returned. The condition for knowing the father's love and joy, in other words, was simply a recognition of need for it and a free, unforced acceptance of it.

We have said that the parable is called the Parable of the Prodigal Son. Its denouement, however, suggests that it might more appropriately be called the Parable of the Elder Brother. The conclusion of the story deals with the behavior of the "good" older brother who had stayed at home and conscientiously done his duty. When the younger brother returned and was so joyously welcomed, the older brother, like the wage-earners in the other story, was indignant. Here he was, the carefully obedient son, who had never wasted *his* substance in riotous living—and no such party had ever been given for him! The father, he thought, was unjust—his love fickle and arbitrary. The older son sulked, because his righteousness-for-reward formula had not paid off. He was reminded by the father that he had the security of the father's home all the time; but his sulking revealed that, unlike the younger brother, he had never recognized love on free and open terms. His jealousy betrayed his true motive for goodness, and his attitude toward his father and brother revealed his incapacity to enter that quality of life which is the life of the Kingdom. He still thought of love as a matter of getting in proportion to giving.

The point of both stories, it seems, is that the Kingdom cannot be *earned,* but it may be *received.* Jesus frequently used grotesquely exaggerated figures of speech, hyperboles, to make his points. Once he said that it is easier for a camel to go through the eye of a needle than for a rich man to enter the Kingdom of God. Everyone was amazed to hear this, because it was generally assumed by the Jews of Jesus' day that riches were a sign of goodness; if a man were wealthy, he must have deserved his wealth, in the strict divine economy of cause and effect between righteousness and prosperity. If a rich man could not be saved, then who could, the disciples asked? "With man it is not possible," said Jesus, "but with God all things are possible." Riches are not in themselves good or evil; but those who *trust* in their riches to save them—whether the riches be in the form of money, popularity, intellect, conscientiousness, religiosity—or self-conscious renunciation of all these—cannot know the joy of the Kingdom. "But with God all things are possible."

One day, said Jesus, two men went up to the temple to pray. One of them, a Pharisee, "thanked God that he was not as other men." He trusted in the "riches" of his "righteousness," and thanked God that he was righteous. The other man was a publican—perhaps one of the despised quislings who collected taxes for Rome at a profit, and were thus considered to be beyond the pale by most loyal Jews. His prayer was simply "Lord, be merciful to me, a sinner." Which man "went down from the temple justified?" Jesus asked. That is, which man left with the proper relation to God, the *just* relation to the Just One? Not the Pharisee who thought he was good enough in relation to the divine justice, said Jesus; rather it was the despised publican, who was at least aware of his spiritual poverty.

When the Kingdom, the "next age" of fulfillment, fully comes, said Jesus, many who now think they surely

35

"have it made" will not be there, and many who think they haven't a chance will be. Many harlots and sinners will enter ahead of the "good" people. Indeed, those who are "first" in the judgment of many "good people" will turn out to be the last in the judgment of God; and the last will be first. The neat scales of justice and judgment by which men rate themselves and their fellow men may turn out to be quite erroneous when measured against the scale of divine love. Those who go around trying to remove specks of "sinfulness" from the eyes of their fellow men had better first become aware of the log of self-righteousness protruding from their own eye, said Jesus in one of his more grotesque hyperboles. "Judge not, that ye be not judged" by the same standards you apply to others. Who could really stand up under such judgment? Let the wheat and the tares grow together in the field until the harvest, said Jesus. There will be a harvest, and there will be a *last* judgment." There is a truth by which, "in the last analysis," men are judged. But men's attempts to make that judgment for themselves all too frequently result in the destruction of wheat along with the tares.

This is not to say that men are to make no moral judgments, or that it does not matter what men do since the divine love accepts or rejects arbitrarily, anyway. Men are free, and they are responsible in their freedom. They must choose to accept or reject the divine acceptance, and their temporal choices have eternal consequences. Jesus freely used the imagery of his time with respect to places of reward and punishment "after this life," or "in the next age." There will be, he said, "weeping and wailing and gnashing of teeth" for those who do not choose while they can the way of life in the Kingdom. No man is coerced into the Kingdom, and the freedom of men to "go to Hell" if they will is respected by the God who wills their free devotion, Jesus taught. God is like a father, to be sure, in that he desires good for all his children, including the good of their free acceptance of his love. But the ideal father in the Near Eastern society of Jesus' day was the one on whom the entire family was dependent, and whose word was law. He was the final *judge*, as well as the final provider and sustainer. The divine love of which Jesus spoke is not a blur of sentimentality which simply overlooks all distinctions between right and wrong, or between responsible and irresponsible uses of freedom. There is justice as well as mercy in it; judgment as well as forgiveness. But the divine love cannot forgive those who do not recognize a need for forgiveness or want to be forgiven. To do so would be to violate the freedom which is the basis of love. Those who choose the unloving way "have their reward." That is, by calculated dealings with their fellow men they may gain power and popularity. One may play the game so cleverly, even with a person intimately involved in one's life, as to manipulate the other's feelings. Through such a bogus substitute for love one may have the "reward" of *feeling* that he is loved. Indeed, he may gain quite a reputation as quite a "loving" person. But the tragedy of his life consists in the fact that he knows only such rewards as the calculated manipulations of other people can bring. He has never known that fullness of love and fullness of life which Jesus called life in the Kingdom.

Yet, said Jesus, while there is life there is hope. It is never too late to repent—to see oneself as one is, and freely to be oneself in relation to others. Furthermore, the kind of love Jesus taught is so spontaneous and un-self-conscious that many who embody it in their lives are totally unconscious of the fact that they do so. In the Last Judgment which is to inaugurate the Kingdom in its fullness, said Jesus, many will be quite surprised to find themselves admitted, just as others will be surprised by their exclusion. Harlots and sinners may enter before many who think of themselves as righteous. Those who, in moments and acts of spontaneous concern, ministered to the needs of others will find themselves in the Kingdom of love. Was a cup of cold water offered to the thirsty, or were the sick and imprisoned visited in their loneliness? "Even as ye have done it unto the least of these," said Jesus, "ye have done it unto me."

This suggests that, while works of mercy are not means for earning the Kingdom, they are appropriate signs or reflections of life within it. Men may not earn God's love; but having received it they should share it, through love of their fellow men. When Jesus was asked one day which is the greatest of the commandments, he replied "Thou shalt love the Lord thy God with all thy heart, mind, and soul . . . all thy being"; God is the first, and only truly adequate, object of human allegiance and love. But there is a second commandment which is "like unto the first," said Jesus, and is, in effect, its completion: "Thou shalt love thy neighbor as thyself." Love of God, and acceptance of his love, is expressed in love and acceptance of the neighbor—as one who is also accepted by God.

It should be noted that Jesus did not say "love your neighbor and despise yourself." Rather he said "love your neighbor *as* yourself." There is an appropriate self-love and self-respect. Its basis is the love of God for the self, and not the qualities and attainments of the self which have come to it through circumstances—or as the result of the common rationality of men which was extolled by the Stoics. But the basis of self-love is equally the basis of neighbor-love. Love of self and neighbor in the equality of God's love for both is the one moral principle of life in the Kingdom. "On these two commandments hang all the Law and the Prophets," said Jesus. All rules and regulations, as well as all principles for the criticism of rules and regulations, are *relative*—relative to this one law of love. "All the rest is commentary," said Hillel, a rabbi of Jesus' day. This means that all that love demands is "required"—and that all is "lawful" that love permits. And the demands and permissions of love are always relative to the specific requirements of specific occasions—they can never be captured in set rules and regulations good for all cultures and all times.

This point is memorably made in Jesus' famous Parable of the Good Samaritan. A certain man, he said, was going down from Jerusalem to Jericho—along a torturous route which drops some two thousand feet in less than twenty miles, skirting glens and chasms where all too easily one might fall among thieves, as this man did. Having robbed and beaten him, the thieves left him by the roadside half dead. Presently a priest came along and saw him . . . but he passed by on the other side, for what he undoubtedly considered good reasons. Later an assistant priest or Levite also came along and saw him . . . but he also passed by on the other side. Then came a Samaritan, a man despised by all good orthodox Jews of Jesus' day. After the Jews returned from exile in Babylon they decided to exclude from the new "Simon-pure" community of Jerusalem those who had remained during the exile and had intermarried with "foreigners." These latter said that they were also sons of Abraham, and that they had the Law too. So they set up a rival temple on Mt. Gerizim in Samaria, or northern Palestine, and claimed that they were the true worshippers of the Lord of the covenant. The quarrel between the Jews and the Samaritans, in other words, was a family quarrel of the bitterest sort. A member of a First Family of Jerusalem would look upon a Samaritan as less than the scum of the earth, because he was an unclean imposter. But, in continuing his story, Jesus said that the Samaritan had compassion on the robbed and wounded man; gave him first aid; placed him on his own beast and took him to the nearest inn; and gave the innkeeper instructions to take good care of him. He, the Samaritan, would foot the bill. Which of these three was neighbor to him who fell among thieves, Jesus asked? The neighbor whom one is to love as he loves himself, within the context of the divine love for both, is simply the next needy person one encounters—and that means the next person, because all have needs of one sort or another. And he is *neighborly*, he is loving, who ministers to those needs as best he can. It is as simple—and as complex—as that!

"Christianity has moved a long way from the simple ethics of the Sermon on the Mount and the simple courage and kindness of Jesus. Even in the New Testament these got all mixed up with the conviction that he was a supernatural being. What is one to make of the claim that he was born of a virgin?"

No competent historian could deny that the Christian tradition has included many interpretations of Christian ethics, and no Christian would deny that Christians are

40

never as good as their faith. The Christian church, someone has said, does not pretend to be a museum of plaster saints. Rather, it is a hospital for sick sinners whose chief virtue, if they have any, is their awareness of lack of virtue and their knowledge of a Source of healing and forgiveness. But the radical relativism of basic Christian ethics is difficult, if not impossible, to maintain. Men seem to need codes and authorities to which they can appeal. In the course of Christian history some groups within the church have thought that the church should be composed of those who are good enough to belong. Others have translated the simple trust or faith which Jesus taught into intellectual assent to dogma, emotional experiences, or other more specific and manageable formulas. Through all the centuries, however, as the faith has received all sorts of people from all sorts of civilizations and cultures, the basic intent of Jesus' ethical teaching has never been completely obscured. Indeed, it has again and again provided a basis for reformation.

It is also true that in the New Testament the teachings of Jesus are "all mixed up with" narratives which express the conviction that he was not an ordinary man. Whether this means that he was "supernatural" depends on what one means by this term—and that depends on what one means by "natural." One may mean by "natural," that which can be understood according to the laws of science. Holding this view, one may then go on to point out that Jesus is alleged to have done many things that are scientifically improbable. Note that one must say improbable and not impossible, because science attempts to provide explanations in terms of probabilities —the statistical averages which we call "the laws of nature." Then, in applying this judgment to the New Testament narratives, one must go on to recognize the fact that Jews of the first century knew very little of scientific laws in the modern sense of the term. So, when the early Christians told of Jesus doing extraordinary things, they were not self-consciously claiming that his actions were "supernatural" in the sense of being contrary to previously established scientific theory. Indeed, the devout Jew or Christian of the first century understood *all* events, finally, in terms of "the will of God." They thought that some events called attention to the divine will more forcefully than did others.

Certainly the early Christians believed that Jesus called attention to the divine in an extraordinary way, and that he was an extraordinary person. Just how they were to talk about and express their sense of his extraordinariness was, and was to continue to be, a problem. In the pages of the New Testament we see him addressed as Rabbi, Teacher, and Master. Even his enemies, it seems, recognized that they were dealing with a man of unusual ability and power. But when some of his followers, following his death, used the term "Messiah" to express his *radical* "extra-ordinariness," orthodox Jews could only denounce the assertion as blasphemous. Jesus was executed on the charge that he made this claim for himself. We have noted that all Jews thought of the Messiah as the special agent of divine fulfillment in history. There were varying views as to what the agent would be—whether, for instance, he would be a Son of David leading to new political power, or a quasi-divine being descending from the heavens to overthrow the existing order and inaugurate the New Age. That he could come from the family of a carpenter in the northern province of Galilee ("Can any good thing come out of Nazareth?"), and be executed as a traitor and blasphemer, was impious and dangerous nonsense, in the view of most good and intelligent people.

Yet it was just this "nonsense" which the early Christians proclaimed. The total impact upon them of the life, teaching, death, and resurrection of Jesus left them no alternative but to use the strongest term they knew to express his extraordinariness, and that term was Messiah: "God's Anointed." It should be noted at once that in no case did they mean by their use of this term to affirm that Jesus was not a man. Rather, their use of the term expressed a value-judgment as to what *kind* of man he was, and how they thought of him in relation to all other men. The gospels were written by men who were convinced that Jesus was the Messiah; only by analyzing the materials they present can we discern something of the events which led them to this conclusion. The gospels themselves present the conviction, not as a conclusion, but as an assumption. Their intent is not so much to persuade as to announce.

It is in this light that we may understand better the intent of the stories of Jesus' birth. Only two of the gospels—Matthew and Luke—tell anything of Jesus' birth and childhood. That there is no mention of an unusual birth in the letters of Paul, written earlier, or in the other gospels, would seem to indicate that the stories of the virgin birth were not of primary importance in the earliest traditions of the church. In Matthew and Luke they express the conviction that Jesus was Messiah by presenting him as the promised Son of David, born in the city of David. A dubious interpretation of a passage

43

in Isaiah (Isaiah 7:14) had led some to believe that the Messiah would be born of a virgin. If Jesus were Messiah, this prophecy must have been fulfilled, they reasoned. Thus we have the moving and treasured accounts of a special Annunciation to his mother, Mary, and of the wondering and trusting acceptance of the extraordinary expression of divine power and love by Mary and her husband, Joseph. St. Luke surrounds these accounts with moving passages which have become part of the Church's most treasured liturgical possessions: the *Ave Maria* and the *Magnificat*. Surely the basic tenor and mood of the entire narrative is poetic and devotional, and the story of the virgin birth may be more appropriately sung than said. It expresses the fundamental Christian conviction concerning the significance of Jesus, in a language and imagery appropriate to the earliest Christian community. An intelligent reader should not have to be reminded that the early Christians were not convinced that Jesus was Messiah because they thought he was a biological oddity! Parthenogenesis, or "virgin birth" is odd though not impossible, biologists say. The gospel writers were saying something much more profound and con- sequential when they told of Jesus' virgin birth. For a Christian to affirm belief in the virgin birth is not neces- sarily to affirm a conviction about the biological circum- stances of Jesus' coming into the world.

The nativity stories also express the gospel writers' estimate of Jesus in other, moving ways. He was, they believed, a strange Messiah whose power was finally most strikingly revealed in the powerlessness of the cross; they told of a lowly birth in a manger. The mean- ing of his life was perceived by ordinary men, frequently before it was perceived by those of more complex cast;

they told of angels announcing the birth to "shepherds keeping watch over their flocks by night," through the hymn *Gloria in excelsis*. But the wisdom incarnate in Jesus was the fulfillment of man's age-long quest for wisdom, they believed; they told of wise men from the East coming to offer their gifts to the Christ-child. His life was a threat to the established order of church and state; they told of attempts on the part of Herod to destroy the child. But, they said, the Holy Family took refuge in Egypt, and then, just as Israel had come out of Egypt in the first great redemptive act of God, so Jesus the Messiah had come out of Egypt to bring God's redemptive purposes to fulfillment. Some who had waited patiently for "the consolation of Israel" recognized him as Messiah at once; St. Luke puts the *Nunc Dimittis*, another of the Church's most treasured hymns, in the mouth of a devout man, Simeon, who recognized Jesus as Messiah when Jesus was brought to the temple for presentation, "after the custom of his people." The stories of Jesus' nativity, in other words, express a constellation of beliefs about the character and significance of Jesus' life. Their truth is of a variety much more profound that that which men usually call "literal."

". . . or that he performed miracles?"

What is a miracle? "An event which happens contrary to natural law," many would say. But many who say this believe that nothing *can* happen which is contrary to natural law, because "natural laws" are simply ways of talking about how things usually happen. So it turns out that, in this way of thinking, a miracle is impossible by definition. If satisfactory evidence can be presented for the occurrence of an unusual event, then one's under-

45

standing of the natural law involved is simply modified to take account of the evidence. But we must remember that the gospel writers, and most of their readers, did not think this way. Whatever happened, most of them would have said, was ultimately "because of" God. God revealed himself in the regularities of nature as well as in irregularities. He was perceived in the glories of the heavens as well as in acts of healing. Some events called the attention of some people to the reality of God more strikingly than did other events, and these were called miracles, or more accurately, *signs* of God's presence. In the Bible, in other words, a miracle is simply any event which strikingly calls attention to the reality of God. But calling attention involves the state of mind of the attender as well as the event attended to. Interpretation as well as fact are involved—if the two can ever be separated. Elizabeth Barrett Browning observed that "Earth's crammed with heaven / And every common bush aflame with God / But only he who sees takes off his shoes." The gospels say that many people saw, in many of the things Jesus did, the expression of unusual power of some sort. But they differed in their interpretations of the source of that power, and of its meaning. Some said its source was Satan, the Evil One. Others said Jesus' power was indeed the power of God; but did not conclude from this that the one exercising it was the Messiah. The Christians saw Jesus' acts as signs that he was indeed Messiah.

Some of the acts which were especially significant as signs, the gospels suggest, were Jesus' acts of healing. That Jesus was a healer even his enemies admitted, as well as multitudes who turned to him primarily as a healer but would have no part of the confession that he

46

was Messiah. His enemies, recognizing the healing, suggested that he healed by the power of Satan, or Beelzebub. This suggests that disease was attributed to an evil power, and that sickness was bound up with sin, in the mind of Jesus' contemporaries. Many of them believed that there was a quasi-independent power in the world, called Satan or Beelzebub, who was constantly tempting men to disobey the laws of God. Indeed, things had come to such a pass that many of Jesus' contemporaries believed that the world had, at least temporarily, literally "gone to the devil." But the devil's power was limited, they thought, and in God's good time the power of sin—and therefore of disease—would be overcome.

To the charge that he was healing by the power of Satan, Jesus replied, "Can a house divided against itself stand?" Where disease was healed, Satan was overthrown; surely Satan would not overthrow himself! In other words, Jesus looked upon healing as a specific sign of God's power. But if moral disease and physical disease—sin and sickness—were bound up with each other as expressions of turning away from God, the source of moral and physical health, then healing must be predicated on forgiveness. In one story we see Jesus asked to heal a man who is paralyzed. He responds to the request by saying to the man "thy sins be forgiven thee." Many who hear it are scandalized: only God has the power to forgive sins, they say. "Which is easier," asks Jesus, to say "thy sins be forgiven" or "take up thy bed and walk"? That the source of forgiveness is also the source of physical health he indicated by then saying to the man, "Take up thy bed and walk"—and, according to the story, he walked. Restoration of physical health followed the restoration of spiritual health through forgiveness. Again and again the gospels show Jesus saying to one who has been healed, "Thy faith hath made thee whole." The faith, however, was a *response* to something present in and through the person of Jesus, and that something Jesus himself called "the power of God." Thus, most of the healing stories are saying, in effect, that total health or salvation (a word derived from a root meaning health) was and is available to men, *from* God and *through* Jesus and men's response to him.

Where sickness was looked on as a form of separation from God, the source of life and health, death would be viewed as the extreme form of that separation. If God has the power of creation and of judgment, Jesus and his contemporaries believed, then he also has the power of re-creation and forgiveness. Thus, stories which show Jesus restoring to life those presumed dead are, in effect, extensions of the healing stories. They are intended as exhibitions of the power of God, through Jesus, to overcome death itself. It should be noted, however, that they do not suggest that those who are reported "raised from the dead" by Jesus are believed thereby to have attained immortality. Rather, they proclaim the conviction that even the extremity of sickness—death—was temporarily overcome in the case of some who turned to Jesus for aid. The gospels suggest that Jesus' enemies did not dispute the authenticity of reports that he had raised Lazarus from the dead. Such stories were not unusual in Jesus' day. But they disputed Jesus' *authority* to do what he was reported to have done. Later, the Christian community was to affirm that through the crucifixion-resurrection of Jesus himself the power of death had been *permanently* overcome. The risen Christ, they said, was the "*first* fruits of those that sleep." That which was partially manifested through him in the case of Lazarus and others, they said, was wholly manifested in the power of his resurrection.

Of course, not all the stories of Jesus' ministry usually lumped together as miracle stories are stories of healing. Some indicate other ways of meeting human need. Some are almost parables, like the story of his stilling a storm at sea when his disciples were afraid, or his walking upon the water to aid them. The lessons they convey about faith and the power of Jesus to bring courage and peace in the midst of fear and tempest are obvious. A similar intent may be seen in the stories of feeding the multitudes (associated in part also with traditions of a Messianic banquet when man's deliverer appeared?), and of turning of water into wine at a wedding feast. The latter story is probably also associated with the role of wine in Christian worship, and with the theme of fulfillment in the Fourth Gospel where it occurs: the fulfillment of water in wine and of bread in "the bread of life." There is no need to examine all of the varieties of New Testament narrative indiscriminately called miracle stories by the average reader. The point is that each story should be understood as a unit in itself, and in terms of the context in which it appears. Knowledge of first-century Hebrew psychology and theology is essential to any judicious estimate of the significance of the stories. It would probably be impossible, and surely would be unprofitable, to attempt to translate accounts which assume a first-century world-view into concepts appropriate to a twentieth-century world-view.

The stories at least provide valuable insights into the impact of Jesus on his contemporaries. In this connection, it should be noted that none of the stories is of the

49

"stunt" variety; always they show Jesus acting to meet a specific human need. Indeed, there are frequent indications in the gospels that Jesus did not want to be known primarily as a wonder-worker, and that again and again he directed recipients of his aid to acknowledge its Source through the established religious channels. It was said that soon after the beginning of his public ministry he was "tempted" to try to influence men by turning stone into bread, casting himself off the roof of the temple to see if God would save him, or using some other "Satanic" means to gain Satanic ends: namely, "the kingdoms of this world." But the stories of Jesus' temptations end with the indication that he rejected these ways, and chose a much more difficult way to teach, preach, and enact the love of the one he called his Heavenly Father.

"All this business about Jesus' death being a sacrifice for man's sins just doesn't make sense."

The gospels are unanimous in stressing Jesus' death as, in a sense, the most powerful act of his life. Events of the last week, and especially of the last day of his life, are presented in much more detail than other events. And a judgment as to the significance of Jesus' death is one of the key affirmations of the Christian faith. Why was Jesus executed? Many answers have been given, pointing to many sources of opposition to Jesus. The established political authorities, whether a native puppet-king like Herod Antipas of Galilee or a Roman official like Pontius Pilate, would have been disturbed by any mass movement which could even be suspected of having political overtones in this time of great political tension, which was to erupt in open revolt less than a generation after Jesus' death. The priestly hierarchy of the temple would have been scandalized by some of Jesus' denunciations of the commercialism and hypocrisy associated with much of the religiosity over which they presided ("It is written: 'My house shall be called a house of prayer,' but you have made it a den of thieves"); and especially by reports that he had said that he would "destroy the temple, and in three days raise it up again." The early Christian community asserted that the latter saying had to do with his death and resurrection, the body being called "the temple of God's spirit." The Pharisees would be incensed by his attitude toward the law: his free and easy treatment of it, relative to the human need which it was designed to meet, and especially his view that men could not be saved by obeying the law. The Sadducees would resent his siding with the Pharisees in such matters as whether there is to be a resurrection of the dead, as well as his criticisms of the temple-orthodoxy, in which they supported the priests. The Essenes were awaiting a more dramatic Messiah, and they would not have approved of his non-ascetic habits and teachings (he was accused of being "a glutton and a winebibber"). The common people who, according to the gospels, at first flocked to hear him and be healed by him, would be increasingly disappointed that he was not willing to use more dramatic means to gain his ends, or to be primarily a healer and wonder-worker. The mob in Jerusalem on Good Friday would be as fickle and bloodthirsty as similar mobs always are. Probably many of the people composing it were among those who hailed Jesus upon his entry into the city on Palm Sunday.

The gospels say that most of Jesus' closest followers had deserted him by the time of his execution. One of them, Judas Iscariot, betrayed him to the authorities and aided in a quick, secret arrest. Judas was the only non-Galilean among the twelve apostles; perhaps he had slights and grievances to settle. He was presumably treasurer of the band; perhaps he was fed up with Jesus' attitude toward money and the necessities of life. Or, perhaps Judas really believed that Jesus was the Messiah, and that by forcing an arrest he would speed up the action, which would surely result in some stupendous display of Jesus' powers and the inauguration of the Messianic Age. Judas' motives remain obscure, as do finally all the motives which led, individually and collectively, to the execution of Jesus. The religious charge against him was that he was a blasphemer; the political charge, that he was a traitor. He was executed by "good" people, representing the best interests of a great religious tradition and an enlightened political power. But, in the last analysis, no religious, political, ethnic, or other group was primarily responsible for Jesus' death. Offended pride; disappointed hopes; evil exposed by love; the need to destroy that which threatens established securities of private and public life—all of these were at work in the execution of Jesus. Perhaps the most profound question to be asked of the event is the one posed simply by a Negro spiritual: "Were you there when they crucified my Lord?"

Many men have felt that they were indeed there—that the forces which put Jesus to death are all-too-familiar ingredients of their daily lives. In the execution of Jesus, they have said, they can see, more powerfully and more dramatically than anywhere else, what such forces lead to. The crucifixion of Jesus, in other words, is a judgment upon that which put him on the cross. The old-fashioned theological word for that is sin. Only by seeing the working out of sin in its consequences for the innocent can sin be seen for what it is. But the final exposure of sin—of the pervasiveness and perversity of pride and prejudice, of envy and of fear—is hardly "good news." Indeed, it is not news at all, except insofar as it is the publication of that which men prefer to suppress.

Christians have pointed to the crucifixion not only as an exposure of sin but also as a victory over sin. To put it simply, Jesus took the consequences of the sin that killed him. He took all that the combined powers of evil—including the physical torment of the ordeal itself—could do to him. One saying from the cross preserved by the Christian community may indicate that he also took the experience of "God-forsakenness" which is the last state of human misery ("My God, my God, why hast thou forsaken me?"). Some note that these words begin a Psalm, the 22nd, which ends on a note of triumph. Their tone from the cross, however, is not triumphant. But from the cross came also the word of forgiveness: "Father, forgive them, for they know not what they do." The man on the cross took all that sin could do to him—and forgave it. The final words from the cross, according to tradition, were calm and victorious: "It is finished . . . into Thy hands I commit my spirit. . ." What does the sum-total of these events, and of these words, mean? What final relationship of life to death, of love to hate, is here enacted?

Some would say, "Here another brave man died for his convictions." Like the death of Socrates, the death of Jesus holds up to men for their emulation a courageous devotion to truth and justice. Some modern New Testament critics, believing that Jesus himself thought that some divine intervention would transform impending defeat into a miraculous inauguration of the Messianic Age, would say, "Here died a deluded man—and history passed him by." Many people have said many things about the death of Jesus. When Christians have said that Jesus' death constituted, as it were, a "sacrifice for sin," they have meant at least that none of these other estimates is wholly adequate. Why they used the language of *sacrifice*, and what they meant by it, is something which must be considered further. But before it can profitably be considered, another question must be asked. The gospels indicate that at the time of the crucifixion not even Jesus' closest followers could see in it any victory, sacrificial or otherwise, for anyone except Jesus' executioners. Disciples and enemies alike concluded on Good Friday that "that . . . was *that*." Jesus was done for; it was indeed "finished." So we must next ask:

What about the resurrection?

Christianity began with the conviction of Jesus' followers that his death was not the end of him, but was rather the beginning of his reign in human hearts. Within three days of his death the scattered, disillusioned apostles were proclaiming the astonishing news that the crucified one was risen. Though their hopes that he might have been Messiah were shattered by the crucifixion, they now proclaimed that God had raised him up in a glorious conquest of sin and death. In his resurrection his Messiahship was finally and unmistakably revealed. Now the true character of the good news was understood. Through the life and teaching, only partially understood before, and through the death

54

completely misunderstood on Good Friday, God was speaking his definitive word of forgiveness and acceptance to man. The power of that word was attested in the resurrection. Sin, and therefore death, were not strong enough to overcome the love of God enfleshed in Jesus. The victory of the grave was not the final victory; the sting of death was drawn. The crucified one was the risen and exalted Messiah. With this message the Christian faith was born.

What events evoked the message? Accounts of the earliest resurrection experiences as given in the gospels are presented with an *appropriate* ambiguity. That which they describe was, in the view of those giving the accounts, literally without precedent in human history. No categories appropriate for the communication of any other kind of human experience, therefore, could be wholly appropriate for the communication of this new fact—this fact as startling as creation itself: the fact of a "*new* creation." The experiences as presented in the gospels are not simply experiences of a revivified corpse, an extension of life to one presumed dead. But the risen Christ was at least as real, they said, as the risen Lazarus. Doubting Thomas was invited to touch the wounds, and the risen Christ joined the disciples in partaking of food; he was at least as real as a physical body. Yet his reality was not *simply* that of a physical body. He appeared and disappeared, and his body was the body of victory over death itself—permanent, not temporary, victory. He was the "first fruits of those that sleep." The reality of the victory they said, was attested by an empty tomb. Yet the earliest written references to the resurrection, in the letters of Paul, make no mention of the empty tomb. Paul experienced the risen Christ on the Damascus road. There was light, and there was sound; and there was a crucifixion and resurrection of Paul, as an old self died and a new self, with a new center of orientation and a new life of hope, arose.

Perhaps the most revealing account of the resurrection is the one which tells of two disillusioned followers of Jesus going home to Emmaus after the crucifixion. On the way they were joined by a stranger. When they told the stranger of their hopes that Jesus might have been the Messiah, and of the shattering of their hopes in the crucifixion, he began to interpret for them the scriptural tradition in which they had been nurtured. When they arrived at their house in the late afternoon, they invited the stranger in. Then they shared with him their food; and suddenly "he was made known to them in the breaking of bread." He was the one who had said, "I was a stranger, and ye took me in." He was the one who had said to his disciples, in his last meal with them, as he blessed and broke the bread, "This is my body." In the remembrance of scriptural tradition, in the compassion for the stranger, and in the sharing and breaking of bread, they encountered the risen Christ.

Of crucial importance to the New Testament understanding of the resurrection experience is the Christian interpretation of Jewish scripture, in the light of which the experience occurred and could be apprehended. The stranger on the road to Emmaus prepared the disciples for their revolutionary experience by interpreting the scriptures. The brief accounts of earliest Christian sermons, given in the Book of the Acts of the Apostles, present the crucifixion-resurrection as being "in accordance with the scriptures." The God of Israel, according to this view, was both creator and re-creator. He had brought

56

Israel into being through the creative-redemptive act of the Exodus. In the Babylonian exile Israel had "died"; in the midst of exile, the prophet Ezekiel had a vision of a field of dry bones—could the skeleton of Israel receive new life? To that query Ezekiel replied to the God of Israel, "Thou knowest." Surely the God who had given life once could give it again if he so willed!

New life came in the return of Israel from the "grave" of exile and the restoration of the "body" of Israel in the land of promise. Time after time, however, Israel was threatened with death. During the death-struggle with Hellenism, in the second century before Christ, the vision of a prophet recorded in the Book of Daniel affirmed the ultimate triumph of the God of righteousness over all powers of sin and death. On the day of God's triumph, the prophet said, graves would open and many who had kept the faith and labored for its fulfillment would be raised up in order to participate in the fulfillment. Jesus had said that the day of that fulfillment, the coming of the Kingdom of God, was at hand. In the resurrection of Jesus, the first Christians said, the Kingdom had come. In the crucifixion, the powers of separation from and rebellion against God had done their worst. By the suffering of the innocent one they had been judged—had been revealed for what they are. Jesus had taken, in his suffering, all that sin could do, and he had overcome it in forgiveness. His victory was attested in the mightiest act of the creating and re-creating, the judging and forgiving God—the resurrection of Jesus as the Christ, the Lord of life and the victor over sin and death. This, said the Christians, was the New Exodus, the beginning of the New Covenant.

III

> "The teachings of Jesus are all right, but much of the rest of the New Testament seems to be theological nonsense. . . . It seems that Paul did more than anybody else to transform the simple Christian faith into a theological puzzle. . . . How could God, if he existed, be a man? Or why should the experience of one man be any more significant for the understanding of God than the experience of other men? . . . What in the world does it mean to say that God is both three and one? What's all this talk about a Father and a Son and a Holy Ghost, and yet only one God?"

"The teachings of Jesus are all right, but much of the rest of the New Testament seems to be theological nonsense."

The faith of the people of the New Covenant, or New Testament, was first proclaimed in Jerusalem by Peter and other disciples who had been transformed and brought together by the experience of the risen Christ. For a time the experience was vividly objective. Then there was a change; one day he disappeared into a cloud, ascending, they believed, into Heaven to join his Father in glory. But before the ascension there was a promise that soon his spirit would move among them in a fresh, new, and powerful way. Meanwhile they would keep the faith, and would keep the structure of the twelve tribes of the New Israel by choosing a successor to Judas the traitor.

And so the mission continued, until on the day of the

Feast of Pentecost, fifty days after Passover, a company of those who had come into the New Covenant community were gathered together to celebrate the festival of the giving of the Law to Moses in the inauguration of the Old Covenant. Suddenly they were overwhelmed by a sense of the immediate presence of the spirit of God—now known to them definitively as the God revealed in Jesus, and thus also the spirit of Christ. He whose spirit had come in wind and fire on Mount Sinai now came again, in a mighty wind and with tongues of fire. Caught up in religious ecstasy, they began to speak with new power a message that was understood by Jews who had come for the Passover-Pentecost season from all parts of the Roman empire—Jews who spoke a variety of native tongues. Throngs of these, according to the account in the Book of Acts, were that day baptized into the New Covenant. "And they continued in the apostolic fellowship, and in the breaking of bread, and in prayer."

Soon some of these Christian Jews who had been brought up in more cosmopolitan cultures outside Palestine began to see in the New Covenant a more radical break with the Old Covenant than their Palestinian Jewish Christian brothers had seen. One of them, named Stephen, one day preached a sermon in which he castigated his non-Christian Jewish brethren so severely for rejecting Jesus as the Messiah—just as they had always rejected the prophets who preceded him, said Stephen—that his Jewish audience was moved to violence, and Stephen was killed by stoning. New tensions arose, and many Hellenistic Jewish Christians were forced to flee Palestine. But wherever they went, throughout the empire, they carried the seeds of the new faith and established new communities.

59

Meanwhile, some of the Palestinian Jewish Christian apostles were having doubts of their own about the exact relation of the New Covenant to the Old. Could Gentiles enter the New Covenant? If so, must they first become Jews? And, after they entered, must they obey any or all of the Law of the Old Covenant? Peter, it was said, once dreamed that he saw a great banquet descending from the clouds. Among the banquet foods were things both kosher and not kosher; "clean" and "unclean." Yet in his dream he heard a divine command to eat all of the foods indiscriminately, "for what God has cleansed, you must not call common." The next day Peter was invited to the house of a Roman centurion at Caesarea, a devout man who wanted to hear the good news. "Truly I perceive that God shows no partiality," said Peter in beginning his sermon. At its conclusion, when the Roman asked for baptism, Peter granted it. When he reported his experience to the company in Jerusalem, some of them concluded that the good news was for Gentiles too. But they were not sure just what this meant, and the new community was to go through much soul-searching before the issue was finally settled.

"It seems that Paul did more than anybody else to transform the simple Christian faith into a theological puzzle."

The key figure in the subsequent debate, and a key figure in the growing mission to the Gentiles in Asia Minor and Europe, was a man who was born into a Jewish family in the great university city of Tarsus, at about the same time Jesus was born in Palestine. His given name was Saul. He was educated in the faith of his people, but participated also in the cosmopolitan culture of Tarsus. It seems that his family enjoyed a favorable status, because Saul inherited an honorary Roman citizenship. From Tarsus he went to Jerusalem, perhaps to study for the rabbinate. His understanding of his faith was that of the Pharisees—indeed, he later said that he became "a Pharisee of the Pharisees." His aim, in other words, was to bring all areas of his life under the control of God through meticulous observance of the Law. In Jerusalem he came in contact with the New Covenant community, and he was sufficiently disturbed by its message to participate in the stoning of Stephen.

As his knowledge of the good news increased, Saul found himself in deeper and deeper personal conflict. If the Christians were right, his entire life had been wrong; all the intensity of his religious devotion had been misdirected. Already, it seems, he had come to have some doubts about the adequacy of Law as the path to wholeness of life with God. In the Law he could discern plainly enough what he ought to do in order to be a true Israelite; but the law did not enable him to do it. Indeed, he perceived within himself a powerful and subtle spirit of rebellion. As Saul's quest for righteousness intensified, he was led to cry out, "The good that I would I do not, and the evil that I would not, I do. O wretched man that I am, who shall deliver me from the body of this death?"

The answer came as he was on the road to Damascus, where he was going to seek out and turn over to the Jewish authorities those who were preaching the new way, which was for Saul at once such a great threat and such a fantastic hope. Insight came in a blinding flash, as he heard a voice ask "Saul, Saul, why do you persecute me?" The voice was identified as the voice of the risen Christ. In this experience of the risen Christ Saul himself underwent a "crucifixion." He was carried almost lifeless to Damascus, and after three days he "rose" to a new life, under the ministering guidance of the Christian community there. From that time on, he said, he was a "new creature." He lived—he lived more fully, more freely, and more completely than he had ever lived before; "and yet not I, but Christ lives in me," he said.

Saul now became as zealous a proponent of the new way as he had been a persecutor of it. The new community was at first suspicious of him, but an apostolic council in Jerusalem was convinced that his experience of the risen Christ was authentic, and that his life was authentically new. With their blessing, then, he was sent off on preaching tours in Asia Minor and, eventually, to Europe. He came to be called by the Roman form of his name, Paul. Typically he would enter a city of Asia Minor and begin a preaching campaign in the local Jewish synagogue, proclaiming the fulfillment of the Old Covenant in the New. Sometimes he would gain a few converts, sometimes many. Often the new congregation would build a new synagogue, and worship not only on the Sabbath, the seventh day, but also on the first day of the week, the day of the resurrection. Increasingly Paul's greatest success came, however, not with his Jewish brethren but with Gentiles who were attracted to the new way. It seemed clear to Paul that these should be directly incorporated into the new community through baptism, and that it was not necessary for them to undergo circumcision before, or to observe the details of Torah after, baptism. He soon found himself in conflict with the Jerusalem Christian community on this matter.

Throughout the rest of his ministry Paul was in constant conflict with Jews, with conservative Jewish Christians, and with those who had vested interests in the practices of Greco-Roman polytheism. Wherever his Jewish-Christian monotheism gained a foothold in Gentile communities, the sale of images and participation in various aspects of polytheistic worship declined. Those who suffered financial or other loss thereby were quick to charge Paul with atheism. Civil authorities often entered the conflict because of their concern over disturbances of the peace. Thus Paul moved from city to city in Asia Minor, and finally over into Macedonia and through Athens to Corinth, propelled both by opposition to his message and by his burning desire to spread it among as many peoples as he could. After he had established little communities he would frequently write letters to them, giving them further guidance in the understanding and practice of the faith. Soon, churches began to collect some of these letters, and finally they were combined with the four gospels and with other letters to form the scriptures of the New Testament.

By A.D. 55 Paul was expressing a desire to go to Spain, which suggests that this was one of the last remaining territories in the Mediterranean world to which the good news had not been carried, less than twenty-five years after the execution of Jesus. First he would visit a Christian community already established in Rome, and before that he would go to Jerusalem to take an offering for the relief of the Christian community there, which was experiencing famine. He would also make a final attempt to heal the breach between the Palestinian Jewish Christians and the Hellenistic Christians on the matter of the role of the Law in the new faith, by taking along a living example of Gentile Christianity, one of his converts. In Jerusalem, however, he was arrested by the Jewish authorities for bringing a Gentile into a forbidden area of the temple, and was turned over to Roman authorities for trial. After a series of delays he revealed his Roman citizenship and demanded trial before Caesar himself, which was his right. He suffered shipwreck en route to Rome, but he finally arrived in the imperial city, and there he spent most of the remaining years of his life. He was kept for a time under house arrest, but was free to receive and instruct visitors and to write letters to churches he had established. There is a strong tradition that he was martyred during Nero's persecution of Christians in Rome in A.D. 66.

This brief summary of Paul's background and career may serve to indicate that whatever theological puzzles he may seem to pose in his letters are the result of his attempt to talk in the language of his day about vital personal experience. Theological language is always, at least in its inception, rooted in human experience. Many have never taken the trouble to find out what experiences those who first used traditional theological terms wished to communicate through these terms. Consider the question formerly posed, as to how Jesus' death could be looked upon as a sacrifice for man's sin. Perhaps we can now see that such an interpretation of the death of Jesus presupposes a view of sin as separation from or rebellion against the source of free and authentic life—called, in the Biblical tradition, "God." Talk about sin will not be intelligible to one who has no sense of lack, no sense of life's being at cross-purposes, no sense of self-defeat. The question is whether there is or ever has been such a person. We have noted that many faiths, ancient and modern, are designed to cover up that reality in human life which the Bible calls sin.

Similarly, to speak of a man's death as a sacrifice, in

the sense which the early Christians intended when speaking of Jesus' crucifixion, is to assume some understanding of the ancient and apparently universal role of sacrifice in man's religions. In all cultures and in all times, it seems, men have felt that in many respects they were not self-sufficient. They were dependent on powers or a power beyond themselves for their physical being, and for their welfare in events beyond their control. To overcome this gap between what they were and what they wished to be, they have offered sacrifices. By giving the best of what they were and had to the source of all, they have sought to overcome their inadequacies, moral or physical. Additional elements have entered into the practice of sacrifice as a form of religious worship: expression of dependence, adoration of the divine, propitiation of guilt, intercession for specific concerns, the establishment of closer communion with the source of life—all these and other human needs have found embodiment in the drama of sacrifice. In Jesus' own religious tradition the sacrificial apparatus of the temple, with its hereditary corps of priests, was a significant element. Throughout the Roman world into which Christianity spread, sacrifice to the various gods and goddesses of the native polytheism was standard religious practice. It is perfectly natural, then, that those who saw in the life, death, and resurrection of Jesus the definitive clue to the meaning of life—the constellation of events through which a sense of separation from life might be overcome —should speak of the gospel drama in terms of sacrifice. Through his acts of forgiveness and healing, culminating in the act of forgiveness from the cross; through the good news of his teaching about the love of God; and especially through the power over sin and death exhibited in the resurrection—Jesus as a man had overcome the separation of man from God which all men experience. He had, in other words, lived and died in order that the intention of all man's sacrifices might be realized.

But note that in the Christian estimate of the life and death of Jesus there is a radical reversal of the psychology of sacrifice as practiced in other religions. In all other practice of sacrifice the emphasis is on what man must do for deity, in order to appease, or otherwise "get right with" deity. In Jesus' life there was a constant emphasis on what God could do through him rather than upon what he could do for God. And in his teaching the emphasis was upon man's inability to make an appropriate sacrifice of either cultic offerings or moral righteousness in order to overcome the barrier between man and God. The good news, said Jesus, was that *what man cannot do for God, God will do for man,* if man will let him. The early Christians then said that in and through Jesus' life, coming to a focus in the crucifixion and resurrection, God had done for man what man had been attempting to do: had overcome the separation of man from God. God had made a sacrifice for man, since man could not make an adequate sacrifice to God. Here was indeed a new word about God!

Paul drew heavily on the language of sacrifice and redemption in his attempt to say what had happened to him in his encounter with the risen Christ. The language of redemption, like the language of sacrifice, is intelligible only to those who feel some need of redemption— who have a sense of being "sold out," or of being in bondage to forces and habits from which they cannot extricate themselves. Slavery was a very real physical fact in the society of the first century, and physical slavery seemed to provide an apt analogue for the sense of self-defeat, of not being master of oneself and one's life, which is a perennial fact of human experience. Paul had known, painfully and at first hand, the sense of being sold out to pride, and to the subtle powers of self-righteousness. In the midst of his conflict he had cried out, "O wretched man that I am, who shall deliver me from the body of this death?" As the result of his encounter with Chirst, he could say, "I thank God, through Jesus Christ." The life, teaching, death, and resurrection of Christ were the new elements in Paul's history which now made his present experience and hope for the future meaningful. His people had always looked back to the exodus from Egypt and the giving of the Law on Sinai as the past events in terms of which their present and future were to be understood. Even so, they had to make that past *their* past, through ceremonial remembrances and pledges, at Passover and Pentecost and other festivals. Likewise, Paul said that the victory over sin which God had accomplished through Christ must be appropriated in each man's present according to the particular structures of his personality. Paul made the crucifixion-resurrection of Jesus his own when he underwent a traumatic change of character-structure on the road to Damascus. The old calculating, bargaining, self-justifying self was painfully destroyed; a new outgoing, free, gracious self emerged. But each man, Paul said, must "come to Christ" in his own way—or rather allow Christ to "come to him" where he is.

One way in which Paul talked about his new life in relation to his old life was in terms of a contrast between "the life of the spirit" and "the life of the flesh." He did not mean by "flesh" the physical body or its needs and pleasures. He was not an ascetic, and he did not think of men as dualities of body and soul, as many Greeks did. He was thoroughly Hebraic in his view of men as indivisible unities created by God. The body, he said, is not something to be ashamed of or escaped from; it is the "temple of the spirit," and should be made a fit vehicle for the life of the spirit. The life of "flesh" which contrasts with the life of the "spirit" is the life of egocentricity, false self-sufficiency, and anxious self-justification. The life of the spirit—that is, of the "spirit of Christ"—is the life of openness, of freedom, and of love. The "fruit of the spirit," said Paul, is "love, joy, peace, longsuffering, gentleness, goodness, faith. . ."

But what *is* this "love" which is the "fruit of the spirit?" Paul attempted to characterize it in one of his most celebrated passages, the Hymn to Love in 1 Corinthians 13. It is, he said, the ingredient without which all beliefs and actions of the religious life are empty and futile. Men may have "faith sufficient to move mountains," and may give all that they are and have for others; but if they are motivated in all this by anything less than love, these things will not bring the quality of eternal life for which they long.

The difference between a life of love and a life without love is the difference between maturity and immaturity. Childish ways are appropriate for children, said Paul, but one cannot know the fullness of life until he "becomes a man" and "puts away childish things." Childishness in an adult is characterized by impatience, jealousy, boastfulness, arrogance, and rudeness. The child naturally insists on its own way, and is frequently irritable and resentful. Love, the way of maturity, is "patient and kind

. . . not jealous or boastful; is not arrogant or rude . . . does not insist on its own way; is not irritable or resentful." It "does not rejoice in the wrong, but rejoices in the right." Love can "take it": it "bears all things." In the midst of all the complexities of life it maintains a steadfast and courageous trust in life—it "believes all things." It never sees life as hopeless, and thus it "endures all things." The one who knows the life of love is the one who has put away childish things. Part of his maturity is his recognition of the inadequacy of his knowledge and of his wisdom. But the knowledge and confidence which life *has* brought result in a faith that, though "now we see in a mirror dimly," there will be a time when we shall have unclouded vision—"shall see face to face." To understand maturely is to know that one "knows in part"— but it is also to have confidence that one "shall understand fully, even as I have been fully understood." Paul felt that he had been fully understood, and had gained self-understanding, through his participation in the drama of the gospel. Three things *last* in life, he said; three things "abide": faith, hope, and love. "But the greatest of these is love." Paul believed that it is literally "love that makes the world go round," and that it is love that outlasts all else. But the love of which he spoke is a much richer and tougher, a much more profound and more mature phenomenon than that extolled in the romantic gospel of minstrels, ancient and modern. It is, he said, "the love of God" made concrete, en-fleshed or in-carnate, in "Jesus Christ our Lord." Paul attempted to sing the glories of that love in his memorable hymn; but, like all other Christians, if pressed further to say what he was really talking about, he would not talk or sing but point—to a man on a cross.

Love engenders not only faith but also hope. It points not only backward but also forward. Paul was hard pressed to spell out the nature of his hope for the future, and especially for that climactic event of everyone's future which is death. He seems to have shared for a while the early Christian hope that the "new age" of which Jesus had spoken would break in upon the "present age" at any moment, and he counseled his charges to live accordingly. Gradually he came to see that "times and seasons" are of secondary concern in the basic Christian hope. While world-history may continue indefinitely, it is by that which was en-fleshed in Jesus that world-history is finally judged. And the life-history of each individual has a certain end: death. When men die, said Paul, they are really dead. There is no inherently immortal soul in man which survives the death of the body.

But recognition of the fact of death does not mean the end of hope. The Christian, said Paul, has experienced in this life a victory over that "body of death" which is the life of anxious self-justification and fear. He has already known a death of this "old" life and a "rising" to "new life." His creator and judge has come to him as also his re-creator and redeemer. On the strength of this experience, Paul could proclaim that the victory which death seems to gain is a hollow victory. Men fear, not dissolution, as the Epicureans maintained, but meaninglessness. If the last word about life is that which is known in the kind of life Paul called "the life of the flesh," then death is a fearful thing indeed. But the Christian's victory over that kind of life, Paul said, removes the sting of death. The Christian knows a quality of life which makes the question of living or dying a secondary question. "Whether I live or die," said Paul, "it is unto the Lord."

The Christian life is lived in a context which embraces and sustains all the facts of living *and* the fact of dying. "I have learned, in whatsoever state I am, to be content," said Paul. He did not mean by this what either a Stoic or an Epicurean might have meant had he said the same thing. He meant that he knew a quality of life, a basis for living, in his relation to Christ, which put everything in life—including death—in its place. "I am persuaded," he said in the eighth chapter of Romans, "that neither death, nor life"; nor any of the forces of good and evil encountered in life—"nor angels, nor principalities"; neither present perplexities nor fears of the future—"nor things present, nor things to come"; neither the heights of exaltation and bliss nor the depths of despair and depression —"nor height nor depth"—"will be able to separate us from the love of God in Christ Jesus our Lord." Those forces which would destroy the meaning of life are "creatures," and neither these nor "anything else in all creation" can overcome the sustaining power of the creator and re-creator of life. To see them as creatures is to put them in their place.

Of course there were those in Paul's day, as there have been in all the Christian centuries, who wished to have this hope spelled out in more concrete terms. They ask, what will the future beyond death be like? What is the furniture of Heaven and the temperature of Hell? Paul called people who ask such questions "foolish," but he patiently tried to answer them as best he could, in passages like 1 Corinthians 15. He tried an analogy from agriculture, and pointed out that the "body" of wheat differs significantly from the "body" of the seed from which it comes, yet there is continuity and identity, and without the sowing and "death" of the seed there can be no "rising" of the wheat. There are "bodies" appropriate to various states of being, terrestrial and celestial, and each body has its appropriate "glory." Man cannot spell out the glory of the "resurrection body" of hope. In talking of such matters he is obviously beyond his depth. But, on the basis of the victory known in this life, he can suggest, said Paul, that "what is sown is perishable, what is raised is imperishable . . . Sown in dishonor, it is raised in glory . . . Sown in weakness, it is raised in power." Man is inherently mortal; but if the creator and re-creator so wills, "this mortal may *put on* immortality." Eternal life, which is not man's natural possession, may be "added to" man.

It was Paul's conviction that precisely this had happened already, in the new life which had been added to his life and the life of the world through Jesus Christ. It was with this faith and this hope that Christians like Paul set out to tell the good news throughout the world. Like Paul, they used idioms derived from their native cultural and religious traditions. They were talking about things that had happened to them, in the depths of their experience, and that had made literally "all the difference in the world" to them. Awareness of this fact is the first requisite for making some sense of the "theological puzzles" of the New Testament and all subsequent expressions of the Christian faith.

"How could God, if he existed, be a man? Or why should the experience of one man be any more significant for the understanding of God than the experience of other men?"

One should note first that this question assumes a

meaning for the word "God" which makes "God being a man" seem nonsensical. The word "God," of course, has many meanings, and most of those who use it to indicate an object of either belief or disbelief probably vacillate in their usage between various meanings, all of them ill-defined. The fact that the question here posed includes the phrase "if he existed" indicates that if there *were* a God in the sense intended by the questioner, he would, in some sense, "exist." Yet most of us probably think of existence as the sum-total of all that is in space and time. To exist, we would say, is to occupy position in space and time. Thus to prove the existence of something or some-one would be to point to it or him in space and time, di-rectly or indirectly; or to adduce facts which in turn would seem to point to the existence in space and time of the person or thing in question. But to use the term "ex-istence" in this manner for God surely seems inappro-priate, both for the believer and for the unbeliever. If there is a God, the unbeliever probably says, he—or it—surely could not be one thing or person among other existing things or persons. God must be "higher" or "more" than that. And the monotheistic believer would probably agree that worship of existing things or persons in "creation" is idolatry. We must ask later just what sense of "existence" the believer has in mind when he affirms that God does exist.

Meanwhile, note that the questioner is implying that, whatever God may be, he is not a man. The word "God," he probably feels, must stand for something "higher" than a man, if it stands for anything at all. Perhaps it is assumed that "God" is the word for an "explanation" of all that is; if so, then surely God could not be a man! More likely, it is assumed that "God" stands for *values*

73

rather than for *facts* or *a* fact. People use the word "God" for that which they believe they are responsible to, and which they believe to be most worthwhile, or worthy of their allegiance. The Christian would share this view with the non-Christian insofar as, for both, "God" stands for that which is of supreme value. Some nonbelievers would probably say that they could understand this use of the term, though they would have good reasons for not using it themselves. But, understanding it in this sense, the nonbeliever might go on to say that he cannot see how anyone could say that a *man* is that which is of supreme value. Perhaps *men* are, or "man-*hood*," the humanist might say. It is more likely that he would say that it is "humanity" as an ideal—as a term for all the "*humane*" values that men should prize and exhibit in their relations with each other—rather than humanity as the sum-total of all people, which may be worthy of religious devotion. In other words, *it is the abstract rather than the concrete* which is held to be worthy of devotion. Men in particular, or humanity in the mass, are too "human" for this!

Leaving aside the ambiguities in the use of words like "human," "humanity," and "humane" thus indicated, let us pursue the fact that the poser of our question seems in any case to be saying that the word "God" must stand for something abstract and universal rather than concrete and particular. There are probably many reasons for his feeling this way. For one thing, he might feel that if the word "God" is to have any explanatory value, then one must turn to science, man's most successful way of explaining things, to see what explanation is. And we note that in science we move from the particular to the universal law which it presumably exhibits when we "explain" the particular. We abstract from the particular that which it has in common with other instances of the same thing. We name it, by putting it in a class—classifying it—and we explain it by showing how its behavior relates to the behavior of other things. To understand a person scientifically is to show all the ways in which he is an instance of various physical, biological, psychological, and other laws. The perfect scientific explanation would be expressed in the most abstract of all languages—the language of mathematics. Therefore, if "God" is supposed to explain anything, then God must be the purest abstraction! Or if the word is understood to be an expression of the *value* of explaining things, we could substitute "Truth" for "God."

Similarly, if "God" stands for moral values, then it must be for these values as principles to be embodied in specific actions, rather than for specific actions themselves. Or perhaps one could use the term "God" for moral values in general and call him (or it?) "Goodness." Likewise, one might consider man's experiences of beauty and think of God as Beauty—in general, but not any particular beautiful thing. Finally, one might stretch his imagination to the breaking point and try to think of God as the one supreme source of *all* values, and yet as somehow "beyond" even these. And this is precisely how many men in many traditions have thought of God. Whatever God may be, they have said, he is not a man— indeed, he *cannot* be, by definition!

When such people hear Christians using language about Jesus which seems to be saying that Jesus is God, therefore, they naturally conclude that Christians are uttering nonsense—that they are expressing contradictions in terms. The only way in which one could make

75

any sense of the Christian affirmations, they would say, would be to take them as statements which affirm that Jesus perfectly—or pre-eminently—embodied and exhibited such abstract values as truth, goodness, and beauty. Then one might go on to say that he was a very good man indeed, (though he said some very bad things about Hell, and there seems to have been an element of vindictiveness in his judgment upon those who did not agree with him or would not believe in him). The "love" that he talked about, some would say, was either too soft and sentimental, or it was inconsistently harsh, in its relation to justice. One might pick and choose from his teachings some very admirable "moral principles." But it would be noted that he was obviously limited in intelligence; he believed in good and evil spirits, and he probably thought the world was coming to an end any day. Surely he did not have a very keen analytical mind! And, while he said some nice things about the lilies of the field, and how Solomon in all his glory was not clothed like one of these, in general he seems to have indicated very little sensitivity to beauty. In other words, to say that Jesus was God, even in the "understandable" sense of being the supreme embodiment of all the abstract values for which the term "God" presumably stands, seems to many to be narrow or naïve, or both.

But the early Christians did not approach the matter in this way. They were heirs of a people who habitually thought, not in abstractions, but in concrete historical terms. In the scriptures of the Jews there is practically no analytical or philosophical thought. Life for them consisted of the immediate and the particular. For their understanding of God they turned not to the regularities of nature or the values of human experience but to the flesh-

and-blood drama of their history. They saw God at work in specific events: the exodus from Egypt, the economic or political affairs of the kingdom,the exile in Babylonia, a specific act of healing, a concrete failure or success. God came to them, they thought, in the "time of their lives." He was the author of, and chief actor in, their history, and of all history. He was to be seen in the personal relations which constitute the human story. He had come in definitive historical events of the past; he was at work in the historical ambiguities of the present; he would come fully and triumphantly in a future conclusion of the historical drama.

If God is known primarily in history, then he must be known in specific histories of specific peoples. History is not abstract or universal; it is specific happenings to specific peoples at specific times. The Jews were convinced that for reasons known to God alone (or for no reasons where reasons are not necessary) they had been chosen as the specific people through whom the meaning of the histories of all other people was to be revealed. They were not chosen because they were better than other people, and they were not chosen to "lord it over" other people, their prophets reminded them again and again. Rather, they were chosen to be the "servant of God," through whom his ways could be made known to all men. Many, we have noted, thought that this service would be completed by a *specific* servant, the Messiah.

The early Christians proclaimed that Jesus was this Messiah. Their Jewish compatriots knew what they were talking about, but they disagreed violently with the judgment. They knew that the Christians were not saying that Jesus was the creator of heaven and earth; or that they had concluded, after careful reflection, that he perfectly embodied the virtues of truth, beauty, and goodness. They knew that the Christians were expressing a personal response to a concrete historical person, and that they were using the most appropriate term they could think of to state their estimate of this person. The Jews understood the term, but they thought the Christians were using it in a ridiculous and offensive manner when they applied it to Jesus. The Jews had not looked for a suffering Messiah, a carpenter's son from Nazareth. Certainly they had not looked for one whose life and teaching would call radically into question the prevailing orthodox formulas for man's relation to God.

And then the early Christians were soon trying to communicate their faith to people who did *not* know what "Messiah" meant. They translated the term into the Greek "Christos." Like "Messiah," this meant "anointed," and referred in the Hebrew tradition to kings and prophets who had been specially anointed to be special agents of God's purposes. In Palestine and other semi-desert countries anointing one's head with oil has a practical purpose well known to all users of sun-tan lotions. Gradually it came also to be a matter of etiquette, and then to take on ceremonial significance. But many Greeks and Romans who heard the Christians saying that Jesus was "Christos" must have thought they were saying simply that Jesus had an oily head—and that seemed a strange reason indeed for worshipping him! So the Christians had to try to explain the Messianic tradition, or to find other words which could communicate to their non-Jewish audience their sense of the significance of Jesus. One such term, widely used, was "Lord."

It is perhaps difficult for a modern person, especially one reared in a democratic culture, to have a sense of the meaning of the word "lord" for those who lived in traditional monarchies or feudal systems, where slavery and serfdom were part of the very texture of society. A lord in such a society was one on whom one was finally dependent, and to whom one finally belonged. The lord was the recognized final authority for one's life. Some gods of other religions, particularly the so-called mystery religions of Greece and Rome, were sometimes called "lords" by their devotees. The Jews had spoken of their God, Jehovah, as their one and only Lord. Here, then, was a word which offered a possible point of contact. The Christians could proclaim to their Gentile neighbors their conviction that Jesus the Christ was Lord—that is, that it was to him that they finally belonged. To him they gave their supreme allegiance; in him they found definitively the meaning of their lives, and the meaning of life for all men. This is why they came to be called "Christians" or "Christ's ones"—that is, those who belong to Christ, who recognize him as their Lord.

Both "Christ" and "Lord" express value-judgments about Jesus. But these are not value-judgments which come to Christians at the end of philosophical reflections concerning the extent to which Jesus embodied in his life such abstractions as love and goodness. They are rather the spontaneous affirmations of men and women responding to another person, in his totality and in his concreteness as a person. The first ones to respond this way to Jesus were some—but by no means all—who had known him in the flesh. They, in turn, communicated the story of his life to others; and some of them, like Paul, said they knew him as directly as the original eye-witnesses, "though not after the flesh." Millions of Christians through two thousand years of history have made the same affirmation.

Those who pose the question to which we have been addressing ourselves perhaps assume that "Lord" is a synonym for "God." And, prizing the abstract and the universal above all else, they may further assume that the word God, if it has any meaning at all, must stand for the quintessence of abstraction and universality. With these assumptions the affirmation, "Jesus is Lord," is indeed nonsense. But even if one sees that "Lord" did not mean "God in the abstract" to the early Christians, one still may ask how one can say that one man is worthy of being called "Lord." How can anybody prove this? Have there not been many admirable and courageous men in the world's history, and might there not be even better ones in the future? How can you know, or how can you prove, that Jesus is the best?

Now the questioner must realize that he is still *assuming* a priority of the general and universal over the concrete and particular. He presumably has in the back of his mind some general standards of excellence which he accepts as worthy of the devotion appropriate for "lords." How does he come by these, and how does he know that these are indeed worthy of his devotion? Are they self-evident to him, and does he assume their self-evidence for others? Leaving aside these crucial questions, one must go on to ask how it is proposed that one apply these general standards to historical candidates for lordship? The task is, as the questioner correctly sees, a hopeless one if one wishes to play the game on these terms. Whether one does or does not is, we suggest, finally a matter of his own basic faith—that which he "takes for granted." We can only point out here that the early Christians did not proceed this way and were not playing the game on these terms when they first confessed that "Jesus is the Christ" or that "Jesus Christ is Lord." When contemporary Christians are faithful to the origins of their tradition they do not play the game on the questioner's terms either. In their confession about Jesus they are actually confessing a different set of rules for understanding some dimensions of life: rules which accord a preeminence to the historical, the individual, the specific, and the personal. Other rules have their place in other forms of understanding, and particularly in that most valuable form of understanding which is called "science." Which rules one accepts as definitive for his personal understanding of personal life, and as the basis of his faith for living, is finally a matter of personal decision.

This is not to say that Christians did not, and do not continue to have on their hands, the problem of the relation of Jesus, as Lord of their lives, to the mystery of creation, and to other men and movements through whom truth is known, beauty perceived, and goodness advanced. They also use the word "God" in talking about these matters. How is Jesus as the Lord of their lives related to God as creator and sustainer of the world, or to the prophets and sages of his own tradition and others? It was to these questions that early Christians were addressing themselves when they evolved the doctrine of the Trinity.

"What in the world does it mean to say that God is both three and one? What's all this talk about a Father and a Son and a Holy Ghost, and yet only one God?"

Moderns may think it strange that the chief problem of the early church in communicating its estimate of

Jesus was not in affirming his "divinity," but in steadfastly maintaining his *humanity*. Yet, in the light of our previous observations about what most moderns usually mean by the word God, perhaps this is not so strange after all. Like us, many people in the Greco-Roman world assumed that God *must* refer to something or someone far above the human and the historical. They could conceive of a series of links between God and man; but that God could be fully incarnate in a man seemed incredible. So, some thinkers who came to the Christian faith from Greek philosophical backgrounds began to say that Jesus was neither really God nor really a man, but something in between. Some of them, called Seem-ists (*Docetists*) said he only *seemed* to be human, but that the "real" Christ did not suffer and die. (It is interesting to note that the Qu'ran, the scripture of Islam, also affirms this view of Jesus. God, the Moslems say, could not possibly suffer!) Others said that Jesus was a superhuman teacher who imparted secret wisdom (*Gnosis*) to those who could understand him, and that this wisdom would lift them above the finite world and guarantee a blissful immortality. They were called Gnostics.

The church rejected both of these views, but not without a struggle. In the early fourth century a priest of Alexandria named Arius began to say that "The Son," or the expression of God in Christ, was a "creature"—but the "first" of all creatures; that is, that the Son was a little lower than God and was created by him, though he was not really a man. Now the term "Son" had been used as an estimate of Christ since New Testament times. The fourth gospel, especially, refers to Jesus as the Son of God. This does not mean that Jesus was thought to be biologically descended from God; nor does it mean that all men are not, in a sense, "sons" of God as equally his creatures and equally recipients of his love. Rather, the fourth gospel uses the term "Son" to say that Jesus perfectly expresses the ideal of "*Son-ship*" in relation to God, whom he called his "Father." The ideal son, to the ancient mind, was one who perfectly obeyed the will of the father, and perfectly embodied the purposes of his father in his life. Sometimes we say of someone that "He is a true son of his father," meaning "he is 'just like' his father, in so many ways." Or we say "he is the very image of his father," meaning "he looks just like his father." In both cases we mean that the son is one through whom the father may be known; we "see" the father in and through the son. It was something like this that the early church had in mind when it referred to Jesus as the true "Son" of God.

But Arius felt that even a true Son of God had to be something "less" than God. God was too far above man for it to be otherwise. This is why he said the "Son" was "created." Arius' bishop, Alexander, saw that Arius' view threatened the very essence of the Christian message: that God really and truly was "in" Christ, "reconciling the world unto himself." To settle the dispute, the Emperor Constantine called together a council of all the bishops of the church throughout the empire, to debate and express the mind of the church on the matter. The council met at Nicaea, in 325. After lengthy debate the council affirmed that "The Son" was "not made"—is not a creature. Yet those aspects of God which are expressed in the word "Son" differ from those aspects expressed in the word "Father." So they said the Son was "begotten"— "before all worlds." That is to say that there never was a time when God was not the kind of God whose nature

83

was revealed to men through Jesus as the Son; he was not first one kind of God and then another. In other words, the nature of God did not and does not change with man's changing understanding of him. God was and is always the love manifested in the Son, though men did not always fully understand him that way. The nature of God's love, the church says in the Nicene Creed, was made known to man when the eternal love of God ("The Son") "was made man" in Jesus. The historical *Jesus*, in other words, was not "begotten before all worlds"; nor is he the creator of heaven and earth. He was truly a human being, who was born; suffered; was crucified under Pontius Pilate; was dead and buried. Here is an affirmation about the nature of God which contains within it a date in history!

But the meaning of the term "God" as used by Christians is not exhausted in all that may be said of his love ("The Son") as historically en-fleshed in Jesus. He is also, said the bishops of Nicaea, the "maker of heaven and earth," the source of all that is. For his nature as creator they used the term "Father Almighty." As the human father is the creator and sustainer of his children, so the Heavenly Father is the creator of all that is not God. Of course the analogy does not fully hold, because the human father does not really create—that is, he does not bring something into being out of nothing. He is rather an instrument of *re-production* or *pro-creation*. Human beings can create nothing; they can only *produce* or *re-*produce new arrangements of material already present. But human production, say Christians, may be taken as an "image," an imperfect reflection, of true creation, which is the work of God alone. Dorothy Sayers, the distinguished novelist, translator and poet, has strikingly called attention to the work of the creative artist as a clue to or image of the true creativity of God in a book called *The Mind of the Maker*. The Council of Nicaea said that "God the Father Almighty" is creator of all that is, and that Jesus as his "Son" is a perfect image or reflection of God's love.

Note that Nicaea stressed the fact that God is the creator of *everything* that is not God. It was important to do this because there were many in the world to which it addressed its findings who believed that God was not the creator of some things, such as "evil" or "matter." This was another reflection of the view that "God" and "good" are words which can refer only to a "spiritual realm," and that the "material" aspects of life are somehow to be ignored or overcome if one is to achieve spiritual perfection. The Christian church affirms that *all* of creation is in principle good, because it is the creation of a good God. It may be distorted from its original goodness, but inherently and naturally it is good. Someone has said that Christianity is the most materialistic of all religions, because it affirms the divine origin of matter and proclaims that matter was a fit vehicle for God's revelation: he was "made flesh and dwelt among us;" the only-begotten Son *was made man.*" In other words, in all that they said about God as "Father" and as "Son" the early church wished to affirm at one and the same time God's deity *and* his full involvement in human history through the incarnation.

Christians use the word "God" not only for the creator of heaven and earth and the love incarnate in Jesus, but also for all creative and revealing men and events of history. The Biblical word for God in this latter aspect is "Spirit." In the Bible the "Spirit of God" or "Holy Spirit" is God's knowable activity in the world—God at work in the world in all the ways not specifically included in his incarnation in Christ. Indeed, the first chapter of The Book of Genesis suggests that it is through the Spirit that the work of creation itself is done ("The Spirit of God moved upon the face of the waters. . .") It would be more accurate to say that it is through the Spirit of God that creation becomes his knowable activity. It is this sense of "Spirit" that is foremost in the Old Testament's emphasis on the Spirit of God, or Holy Spirit, as the agency through which the prophets were able to discern the signs of their times. The prophets' gifts of insight, in other words, were "gifts of the Spirit." The gospel writers used the word in this sense when they affirmed that it was "through the Spirit" or "in the power of the Spirit" that Jesus did what he did. Then, at the Feast of Pentecost described in the second chapter of the Book of the Acts of the Apostles, the Holy Spirit (or "Holy Ghost" in the Elizabethan English of the King James Version of the Bible) is said to have "come upon" the early church. That is, the quickening power which had illumined the prophets and sustained Jesus was now known in a definitive way by Jesus' followers. They would now think of the Spirit of God as the Spirit of Jesus.

In the rest of the New Testament the terms "Spirit of God," "Holy Spirit (or Ghost)," and "Spirit of Christ" are used more or less interchangeably. So the Council of Nicaea went on to affirm its belief in God as not only the Father-creator and Son-redeemer, but also Spirit-Lord and life-giver, "who spake by the prophets." And the church knew that God's "speaking" had not ended with Jesus. The very spirit which had animated him could lead men to deeper and clearer understanding of that which he had revealed, and to more and more discoveries of truth, creations of beauty, and achievements of goodness. Therefore Christians may say that wherever a scientist patiently works toward the discovery of truth, or an artist labors to express new beauty, or a statesman or industrial manager or labor leader works for the extension of justice in human affairs, the Holy Spirit is at work.

God, then, said the Council of Nicaea, is Father, Son, and Spirit. But there is only one God. How is one to talk of the three aspects of God in such a way as to maintain their difference while affirming their unitary reference to God? This problem had long bothered the church, and many theologians had suggested various analogies from human affairs which might help to make the point clear. Some said that it was as if God were an actor playing three roles in a drama. This was common practice in the theater of the day; the actor had only to don different masks for each role. The masks or roles were called *personae,* a word which survives in the contemporary term dramatis personae. God, said those who commended this analogy, is one God, but he acts as creator, redeemer, and illuminator. He is three "persons" in the sense of playing three roles, but he is one actor-God. The church thought this analogy was useful but would not accept it without qualification, because it might seem to suggest that there is change in God, as the actor changes roles—that is, that God was first Creator, then Son, and later Holy Spirit. But there is no temporality, no sequence of being, in God. Or the analogy might suggest that God the Father suffered as God the Son—that is, there might be a confusion of roles.

Well, then, would some other analogy do? An ex-lawyer, Tertullian, suggested an analogy from Roman law, in which three people could be common owners of one "property," or, conversely, one person could own three "properties." But this analogy also breaks down if pressed too far. Indeed, words like aspects and expressions which we have been using are not wholly adequate for the sense of unity-in-threeness or threeness-in-unity which characterizes the Christian view of God.

The *experience* which the church wished to communicate at Nicaea and subsequently (and we must never forget that theology is the communication of human experience) is the Christian experience of a God about whom Christians are unable to say one thing without saying three things. The Father Almighty who is the creator of all things is the source of the love made flesh in Jesus as the Son. The Son, in turn, is the Son of that Father, who has *always* been the love made flesh in Jesus. The Holy Spirit is the Spirit of the Son of that Father, and of the Father of that Son. . . . and so it goes. One cannot grasp the Christian affirmation about God at any one point without simultaneously grasping two other points: each implies the other two. Yet each point is distinct from the other two. So the Christian says God is three, yet not three Gods; he is one God who is three*fold*. He is, in other words, a tri-nity.

The Council of Nicaea used the Greek word *ousios*, translated "substance," or that which "stands under" a thing to constitute its reality—its "definition"—to indicate the "common ground" of the Father and the Son. The Arians wished to say that the Son was *homoi-ousios*, "of *like* substance" with the Father. That is, again they wished to pull apart the incarnation by affirming that the love incarnate in Christ is "God-like," but not fully "God" in the sense that "The Father"—the transcendant creator

88

of all—is. But the Council affirmed the incarnation, and said that the Son is *homo-ousios*—"of the same substance" as the Father. That is, the character of love which is "The Son" is as truly the character of God as is the character of "The Father" as almighty creator of all that is.

Latin translations of the Creed used the word *substantia* for the common divine ground of Father, Son, and Spirit, and used the word *personae* for the three distinct expressions of God. In so doing they gave the word "person" a new sense, similar to but yet different from the theatrical sense of "role." Our own use of the term "person" today is highly ambiguous, and we may be just beginning to discover what personality is. Perhaps our vaguely conceived sense of personhood is actually derived from the Christian use of *persona* with reference to God.

The point is that the church had to use words in new ways to say something genuinely new about God. That is what it was doing when it established the doctrine of the trinity. It was literally saying three things at once. The good news was, as it had been from the beginning, that God is not simply the far-off, abstract creator, or unitary source of values; he is also equally the love made flesh in Jesus the Son, a love which could sweat drops of blood and know the agony of the cross; and he is the quickening spirit of creative discovery and achievement which continues to animate the world.

IV

"Christians haven't been satisfied with that—they have added dogma to dogma in long and complicated creeds which people are required to believe. . . . Instead of concentrating on living in the spirit of Jesus, Christians have gotten all involved in the paraphernalia of worship and church organization. . . . All this Christian doctrine sounds nice, but is it logical? It all assumes the existence of God—but can you *prove* the existence of God?"

"Christians haven't been satisfied with that—they have added dogma to dogma in long and complicated creeds which people are required to believe."

The Nicene Creed is the most widely used creed in Christendom. While it contains many more words than those we have quoted in our analysis so far, most of the words refer to the Trinity. The first paragraph of the creed refers to the Father, the second to the Son, and the third to the Holy Spirit. The second paragraph is by far the longest. It was felt necessary to spell out the historical action of Jesus as the Son, and to make as forcefully as possible the point that Christians believe that God really acts in history, and that history is, in the last analysis, judged by his action in Christ (who will "come again to judge the quick and the dead"). The authenticity of this action, says the creed, was made clear in the resurrection of Christ, and Christians look toward a general "resurrection of the dead" and a "life everlasting." We must consider later in more detail just what these terms may mean. The remainder of the creed expresses Christian belief in the unity and universality of the church as a redemptive fellowship. Thus the creed couples a statement about God with a statement about the character of that community which expresses the appropriate human response to God's action in Christ.

It is true that some other creeds, like the so-called Athanasian Creed, are longer and more detailed than the Nicene, and may seem to "add dogma to dogma." They are, however, results of dispute about the meaning of key terms of the Nicene Creed, or of the even shorter Apostles' Creed. The latter was used as a short statement of Christian faith by candidates for baptism as early as the second century, and was taken to be a succinct summary of the faith of the apostles. Thus we see that the making of creeds was not a matter of idle speculation or theological gamesmanship. From the very beginning of the Christian movement, the claim to be a Christian could be literally a matter of life and death. Christians were subject to persecution, first by their non-Christian Jewish compatriots, and then by the Romans. If allegiance to a faith is a matter of life and death, then it is important to be as clear as one can be about just what it is that one believes in!

But the Christians looked upon their faith as primarily a way of *life*, not as a way of death, violent or natural. And it is important to attempt to state as clearly and succinctly as possible the nature of one's faith for living. By the fourth century Christianity had overcome its persecutors and had been established as the official religion of the empire. Suddenly it was more hazardous not to be a Christian than to be one. Being a Christian became "the thing to do," the "smart" thing for those who wished to get ahead in business, government, or society. This state of affairs tended to encourage the view that Christianity could be a very vague matter, meaning different things to different people, so long as they were all "nice" people. In this situation creeds became even more necessary, if Christianity were not simply to evaporate. If it could mean all things to all people it would soon mean nothing to anyone. The lines had to be drawn somewhere, if the faith was to have a continuing identity.

Actually it was heresy that made orthodoxy necessary. The word "heresy" comes from a Greek word (*hairein*) meaning to choose. In other words, "heresies" were theoretically simply views of Christianity which various people chose to hold. Now there is no basis in Christianity for denying people the freedom to choose to believe what they please. The church, of course, was later to act as if it had forgotten this, as belief came to be associated with political policy, and heresy to be linked with disloyalty to authority. A basic affirmation of the Christian faith, however, is that God is love, and that his love respects the freedom of men. Thus men are "required" to believe only that which they can honestly believe, and they are responsible only for what they know, not for what they do not know. We may see that even the most authoritarian groups in Christendom have never quite forgotten this principle as a logical implicate of the Christian faith.

But it is one thing to say that men are free to believe what they choose, and another thing to say that it is all right for them to call anything they choose to believe "Christianity." Matters of fact are at stake here. There were indelible marks of identity for the Christian community from the very beginning. We have noted some of them in our analysis of New Testament faith. There were specific things which made a difference between the Christians' faith and the faiths of others—enough difference to get the Christians killed occasionally. It became increasingly difficult to keep these differences clear as the faith spread among peoples who were committed to a wide variety of alternative faiths. The earliest Christian creed was probably the simple affirmation, "Jesus is Lord." In a small community of essentially Jewish background this simple statement would have been enough to differentiate Christianity from its religious environment. But as the faith was communicated to people who had quite different assumptions about God and man, it became impossible to maintain the original simple affirmation without further clarification. It turned out to be not so simple after all, but to carry with it a view of life and the world which was quite foreign to those to whom it was communicated. One result, with respect to the nature of God in relation to Christ, we have noted. On all sides were people who wished to accommodate the faith to their previous assumptions about God.

By and large, the church looked upon most of the resulting statements as half-truths. Some, though few, wished to affirm the humanity of Jesus in such a way as to deny his uniqueness. The church said he was human, to be sure, but unique in his relation to God. Most wished to affirm his "divinity" at the expense of his humanity. The church said there is a specific sense in which it may be said that Jesus was divine, but that this affirmation does not deny his genuine humanity. And so it was with most of the heresies. In most cases

93

the church did not *deny* what the heretics *affirmed*, but went on to *affirm* some things which the heretics *denied*. To "mainstream" Christians the heresies seemed truncated, narrow, or incomplete versions of the full Christian truth. It was all right for people to hold these views if they wished, but they should not call them "orthodox" (a word meaning "right opinion about") Christian faith. Indeed, the distortions of heresy do not provide fully saving truth, said the church, and half-truth can be more dangerous than patent error. So heresies were anathematized. Note that *heretics* were not thereby affirmed to be "bad" people. They were branded as people who held erroneous views. The *views*, not the *people*, were condemned. Later the church was to act as if it had forgotten the distinction.

Even a relatively complicated creed like the Athanasian cannot be looked upon as a summary of Christian theology, a full statement of Christian belief in relation to all possible distortions or negations of the faith. What we now call creeds were originally called "symbols." They are short-hand statements, as it were, of the minimal essence of the faith, recited by those who wish to pledge allegiance to that faith. Their purpose was and is practical, not theoretical. They constitute "working agreements," as it were. Their language is more dramatic than technical; more poetic than prosaic. They begin, not with the words "I know that . . ." or "I believe that," but "I believe *in*." Originally the "I" was "we"; and the intent is always communal: it is a community, not an isolated individual, that confesses the faith. The isolated individual may speculate philosophically or theologically, and come up with a statement of his view of the world. But the Christian in reciting a creed is not stating his private view of life; he is confessing the faith of a community in which he finds meaning for his life.

The Christian says, "I believe *in*. . ." Contrast the intent of statements like "I know that two and two are four" or "I believe that men will reach the moon within a decade" with statements like "I believe *in* democracy" or "I believe in Dr. Smith." The latter statements involve other statements, like "I believe democracy is a system which provides checks and balances of power" and "I believe Dr. Smith is well educated and conscientious." But "I believe *in* democracy," or "in Dr. Smith" communicates something more. There is an element of commitment or trust involved which in a sense "goes beyond the evidence," and surely goes beyond the implications of the former two statements for one's personal living. To say "I believe in God" is to say "I trust in" that which one intends the word "God" to mean. Christian creeds are attempts to say what Christians think the word "God" means, and to indicate something of the consequence of that belief for the life of the Christian.

It is sometimes said that creeds are better sung than said. While this may not be literally true as a prescription for the way in which creeds should be used in worship, the statement may serve to remind us that creeds are intended *for* use in worship—as affirmations by a worshipping community of what the community holds worthy of worship. All of the dramatic resources of the arts may appropriately be employed to express such affirmations, because all of life is involved in the commitments which they express. It may be that the saying of a creed all too easily suggests that what is being communicated is a matter of prosaic fact rather than momentous truth. The expressions of worship are the expressions of that truth which is *most* momentous for the worshipper. But this observation may lead to the statement that

"Instead of concentrating on living in the spirit of Jesus, Christians have gotten all involved in the paraphernalia of worship and church organization."

It is true that from the beginning Christians were "involved in . . . worship." Worship is the one distinctively religious act. While religions may include beliefs about objects of worship, prescriptions for conduct held to be consonant with these beliefs, and expressions of these beliefs in artistic creations, it is worship as such which constitutes specifically religious behavior. Philosophies include beliefs; there are non-religious forms of morality; and the aesthetic life may be pursued as a good in its own right; but only religion expresses its basic concern through worship. To worship is to acknowledge in a special way that something or someone is worthy of worship. Now some people may hold that there is nothing beyond themselves, or the world, or "man," which is worthy of worship. There is a sense in which it may be said that they worship themselves, or a "cause," or "nature." In the history of religions literally everything under the sun seems to have been an object of worship by some people somewhere.

But even in primitive religions the attitude expressed toward specific objects of worship is something more than a literal holding of these objects as such to be worthy of complete devotion. There is always an element of "transcendence;" a "pointing beyond" the specific object, to the more vaguely felt "other" to which the worshipper wishes to be religiously related through his use of the worship-object. A nineteenth-century German philosopher of religion, Freiderich Schleiermacher, said that religion is rooted in a special "feeling of absolute dependence." Beyond the partial dependencies of everyday life on elements of nature and society, religion says there is a total dependence on that which is beyond all these. Another philosopher and historian of religion, Rudolph Otto, said that the distinctively religious category is an implicate of worship, the distinctively religious act. He called this category "the holy," and he characterized it as "the tremendous and fascinating mystery" (*mysterium tremendum et fascinosum.*) Where there is a sense of the holy there is religion; and where there is religion there is worship, as the uniquely religious expression of the sense of the holy. In all cultures men have made distinctions between the "sacred" and the "profane," and have evolved special ways of expressing relations to the sacred. These ways constitute worship. Perhaps the only person who can have no understanding of what worship is all about is the person for whom literally "nothing is sacred"—if there is such a person.

The worship practices of the early Christians were largely derived from their Jewish antecedents. Judaism provided a rich store of aids to private devotion, in psalms and other forms of meditational literature. In these, the whole gamut of human emotions and concerns was expressed in appropriate religious form. The Jewish sense of the transcendance of God above all created things led to a prohibition of the use of "graven images," lest their use should lead to idolatry. But the aesthetic powers of the Jewish people were magnificently expressed in religious literature. Readers of the Bible should never forget that the chief purpose of this literature, varied in form and expressing a wide range of human concerns, is to relate men to God. Much of it was originally designed to be recited in public worship.

The public worship of the Jews in Jesus' day centered around the temple and the synagogue. In the temple a daily round of sacrifices for all the intentions of the entire people was performed by a hereditary priesthood. Individuals and families could also go to the sanctuary in Jerusalem to express thanks or offer petitions for special occasions and concerns. Of great importance were the annual festivals for all the people, recalling the crucial events of their past through which they had come to know their God. The gospels show Jesus being taken to the temple for the presentation, or dedication ceremony, and St. Luke tells of his accompanying his parents to a Passover celebration when he was twelve years old. He was in Jerusalem to celebrate another Passover when he was arrested and executed. He had some scathing things to say about the perversions and distortions and commercialization of worship in the temple in his day; but he never denounced temple worship *as such*. Like the prophets before him, he seems to have been intent on purifying and reforming this important part of his people's religious heritage.

More immediate and intimate resources for public worship by Jews of Jesus' day were to be found in the synagogues. A synagogue congregation could be organized wherever ten Jewish males wished to do so, and the community life of each village centered in its synagogue. The synagogue was a school, where young and old went to study the literature of the people; it was a community center, where governmental and other community affairs were carried on; and it was a place of worship. The chief times of worship were the sabbath, or seventh, days. On these occasions the people of the congregation would gather to sing hymns, engage in corporate prayer, hear lessons from the Bible, and perhaps hear a sermon by a rabbi—one learned in the scriptures. The gospels often show Jesus at synagogue; one of them says his public ministry began with a sermon in his home church at Nazareth. One of the titles by which he was most frequently addressed was Rabbi.

Now all along we have been referring to the Christian community as the Christian "church," and we have noted that it was the church which was involved in defining belief and evolving forms of worship. But what and where *is* the church, and with what right did the church define the Christian faith? The word "church" is from the Greek *ecclesia,* a rendering of the Hebrew *q'hal,* frequently translated "congregation" or "people." In Jewish usage the term referred to the People of God as a whole—the people of the Covenant. The Christian community first defined itself as the People of the *New* Covenant. It traced its origins to the apostolic fellowship which formed around Jesus and declared its faith through Peter's confession, "Thou art the Christ." This fellowship had gained new understanding of itself and its Lord in the experiences of the resurrection, and at Pentecost it had its "baptism of fire." The "congregation" which was the church as a whole had local embodiment in local congregations wherever the faith was spread. The church in Jerusalem was the "mother church" until the fall of Jerusalem to the Romans in A.D. 70. Jesus' kinsman James was revered as a leader of the Jerusalem church; and it was to an apostolic council in Jerusalem that Paul appealed for ordination to his mission work, and for settlement of disputes which arose in the course of his missions. With the fall of Jerusalem, local congregations looked to their own founding churches, or to the churches of their provincial capitals, for guidance. Antioch, Alexandria, Smyrna, or increasingly and naturally, Rome, were looked to for leadership. Rome was the center of empire; and Rome, it was said, was where Peter and Paul were martyred. Indeed, it was said that Peter himself had founded the church in Rome.

Since the earliest Christian congregations emerged from Jewish congregations, it was natural that their government should be patterned after that of the synagogues. In each church there was a council of "elders" (*presbuteroi*). Frequently one of these was elected president or "overseer" (*episcopos*). As the business and relief-work of the churches increased, it became necessary to appoint other officers to help carry out this aspect of the churches' work; these were called "deacons." The first Christian martyr, Stephen, was a deacon. So long as apostles like the twelve (including Matthias, elected to succeed Judas Iscariot) or Paul were alive, all churches looked to them for definitive guidance in major matters of faith and conduct.

The church needed not only officers of administration but also officers of worship. The Christian synagogues continued the Jewish synagogue practice of gathering on holy days for worship and study. While for the Jews the regular weekly day for worship was the sabbath, or seventh day of the week, for Christians it was the first day of the week, Sunday: the day of the resurrection. In both types of synagogues, lessons from the Jewish scriptures were read and Hebrew psalms were sung or chanted. Following the reading of an appointed lesson, someone learned in the scriptures might deliver an interpretive discourse. The entire congregation would join in appropriate prayers. In Christian synagogues the reading from the Old Testament would be followed by the reading of a recent letter from Paul or some other apostle, or some written account of sayings and acts of Jesus. Soon these accounts of sayings and acts were collected in the four gospels which became authoritative for all churches, and the letters took their place beside them to constitute the scriptures of the New Testament. In other words, most of the Bible itself came out of the church's worship.

From the beginning, the Christian community had also included ceremonial meals as basic features of its fellowship and worship. Some of these meals were simple repetitions of the Last Supper of Jesus with his disciples. Others were more elaborate "love-feasts," to which all members of the congregation brought food and drink to be shared by all. In one of his letters Paul had to warn the congregation at Corinth against unseemly behavior at these covered-dish suppers. People should not start eating until all had arrived, he said, and all should share and share alike rather than picking and choosing from the better dishes brought by the better-to-do. Above all, the flow of wine should be kept under control, lest non-Christians should get false impressions of Christian freedom and liberty.

Gradually the love-feasts and Last Supper celebrations merged into one, central, regular act of worship called "The Eucharist." This word in Greek means "thanksgiving," and the giving of thanks to God for all his works, and especially for his redemptive work in and through Christ, was a basic theme of the ceremony from the beginning. But it included also the memorial repetition of the Supper; prayers of confession, praise, and intercession; and, in the offering of the bread and wine re-presenting the body and blood of Christ, sacrifice. The sacrifice of Calvary was re-enacted in the celebration of the Eucharist. Thus another element of worship—the great drama of sacrifice, found in all religions and present in Judaism in the daily round of temple worship—was incorporated into the central act of Christian observance.

In the liturgical life of the church the elders, or "presbyters," served as "priests." The guardians or overseers, now styled "bishops" (*episcopoi*), were comparable to the High Priests of the Old Covenant. The deacons assisted bishops and priests in the liturgical as well as in the administrative life of the church. With the passing of the apostles, the bishops came to be looked upon as bearers of apostolic authority. And during periods of persecution and internal dispute, the bishops became the spokesmen for the church as a whole. The bishops of churches in provincial capitals or diocesan centers were looked to for guidance and government by the churches in their areas. And the Bishop of Rome came naturally to be regarded as *primus inter pares*. Thus when it became necessary to define the minimal affirmations of the faith, it was a council of 318 bishops from all areas of the empire, meeting in Nicaea in 325, that spoke the mind of the church.

From all of this we may see that the quarrels and disputes which arose in the later history of the church, concerning the nature of the church and the proper forms of government and worship, resulted from attempts to carry forward the early experience of Christians when they first formed themselves into a separate worshipping community. Remember that the word "church" or "congregation" meant in Hebrew the *whole* "People of God." Some Christians were later to feel that the wholeness or "catholicity" of the church as an overarching community might be threatened by too much emphasis on the local congregation. Others were to feel that the local congregation, which had been essentially a lay-organization under local control in Judaism, might lose its autonomy or be swallowed up in the larger "church-as-a-whole" if proper safeguards were not provided. Others were to favor regional organizations of "presbyters" as the basic governing unit. Some would place authority in the local congregations, and others would place it in the bishops, and especially in the Bishop of Rome. Similarly, in the worship life of the church there were those who prized above all else the reading of scripture and the preaching of the Word communicated through scripture. Others prized the Eucharist most highly, as the one great drama through which the entire gospel is enacted. Most Christians down through the years could agree with the minimal definition of the church as the community where the gospel is preached and the sacraments enacted.

In addition to the Eucharist as a sacrament, or sacred action, there was baptism. In first-century Judaism baptism involved the immersion of the candidate in water, and it was required of converts to Judaism. It symbolized a purification and an initiation into a new way of life. John the Baptist in Jesus' day proclaimed that baptism was needed by all, whether they had been born Jews or not. "God can raise up sons of Abraham from these stones if he wills," he said; to be a true "son of the covenant" is not a matter of birthright. Jesus submitted to baptism by John at the beginning of his public ministry, and the gospels say that he commanded his disciples to baptize converts to the new faith of the New Covenant. Their immersion signified their "death" to old patterns of life, and their being raised up from the water signified their "resurrection" to a new life. The rite as a whole constituted their initiation into the church. Later it was felt that total immersion of the body was not necessary to symbolize the basic intent of the rite; causing water to flow upon the body in some manner was sufficient. In later years there would be those who would stress one meaning of the act above all others, or would insist on the original form of its performance, or on one subsequent form, rather than another. But for all Christians it has remained, along with the Eucharist, a concrete act through which one identifies his life with that of the church and its Lord.

It is not true, then, that the church "got involved in the paraphernalia of worship *instead of* concentrating on living in the spirit of Jesus." Rather, the life of worship was seen to be of fundamental importance for those who would seek to live in the spirit of Jesus. And the "paraphernalia of worship" were the ways and means of worship available to the Christian community from their Jewish background, and from their own new life together as the People of God.

"All this Christian doctrine sounds nice, but is it logical? It all assumes the existence of God—but can you prove the existence of God?"

The reader who really wants to raise this question, and wants anything more than a perfunctory answer, must be prepared to do a little hard digging, a little hard reading, if he is to reach any worthwhile conclusions *pro* or *con*. He must stop to ask just what his question really is; how one could reasonably go about answering it; and how one would recognize an answer when he saw one. It is fairly easy to summarize in a popular fashion most of the arguments people give when they are asked to prove the existence of God. The world doesn't explain itself, they say, so there must be a God to explain it. Or some feature of the world, such as its order and design, demands a divine origin to account for it. Others would say that if there were no God it would never have occurred to men to think that there is, and they would then point to allegedly universal belief in deity of some sort. Still others point not so much to man's experience of facts as to his experience of values, and especially moral value, as a kind of experience which can be finally explained only in terms of God as the giver and guarantor of moral law.

Those who find one or more of these arguments convincing may find it useful now to re-examine the matter in the light of some classical and rigorous statements of the arguments. Those who find none of them convincing may find it useful to see if they have fully understood the arguments they reject. We propose here to trace some of the major arguments in some detail, and this will require learning some of the philosophical language in which classical exponents of the arguments have put them. Readers who do not feel that this would be worth the bother may turn on to the next topic.

We cannot examine the question fruitfully unless we have first specified what we mean by such key terms as "prove," "existence," and "God." Those who would insist that the question remains unanswered when one has shown what *faith* in God has meant to sensitive souls, and has described what the Christian faith is, probably mean by "proof" logical inference based on observation of facts. The existence of God would be proved, such people think, only if it could be shown that observed facts in the world logically demand the assertion of the existence of God as their explanation. Or, some might think that the existence of God would be proved only if God himself could somehow be shown to be an observed fact.

It is indeed true that the Biblically oriented Christian faith which we have thus far analyzed takes God, rather than the world or man, "for granted"; and hence there is no attempt in the Bible to prove the existence of God from the existence of the world. In the Bible, the task is to understand man and the world in the light of God's existence. It is interesting to note the development of Western thought which has moved from a God-centered to a nature-centered, and finally to a man-centered, or *ego*-centered, world. To ask that the existence of God be proved in the way the existence of things in the world is proved is to start with the world and its components as something more evident than God. Yet, since we as moderns must ask what can be done if one does start this way, we must see what we can do with the challenge.

The next key term in the question about proving God's existence is the word "existence" itself. For something to exist, most of us would say, it must occupy position in space and time. Thus, if the existence of God is to be proved, then one must be able to show that a being among other beings, called "God," exists somewhere in space and time. A moment's reflection, however, shows that such a God, if he existed, would be of very little religious or philosophical value. He would be just one more thing in the world, related to all other things in a special way. The questions "why the world?" or how and whether one has thus accounted for *existence as such,* would remain unanswered. A being *in* space and time could not account for the existence *of* space and time. Thus many philosophers and theologians have affirmed that God is not one being among others, *in* existence as other things are, but that he is *being-itself,* or that he is that *true* existence which is the "ground" of spatio-temporal existence. In other words, God is literally "no-thing," and he is "no-where." And the only time-concept which could be applied even indirectly to him is the concept of "now." For him there is no past, or future; no "then" and "there"; he is the Eternal Now, the "ground" of all times and places.

But does this kind of talk make any sense? Again we must note that it does not if one *assumes* that the word "existence" must be restricted to locatable things and events. It also makes no sense if one believes that it is not necessary to go beyond locatable things and events in order to account for them. Is it not enough, some would ask, simply to note that things are, and that events happen, without going behind them to something which is neither a thing nor an event in order to explain them? Certainly we do not need to make a move of this sort for scientific purposes. To explain something scientifically is to classify it, and to show how its existence relates to the existence of other things. The question "why anything at all?" is not a scientific question. Matter or energy are said to be uncreated or endlessly created—that is, the existence of matter or energy is *assumed* in scientific inquiry. And there is no *scientific* reason for not making this assumption. Are there other reasons? Does the question "why is there anything at all?" still make a certain kind of sense, or at least *express an authentic human response to reality*, when one has done all he can toward explaining the world scientifically?

There are those who would claim that it does, but that the answer to the question "why the world?" is not "God" in the traditional Christian sense of this term. The existence of any particular thing or event, they would say, needs to be explained by reference to other things and events; and in a way it may be said that in order to explain *anything* you must explain *everything*. Yet might it not be said that, while everything *in* the world depends on everything else in the world for its existence, "the world as a *whole*" depends on nothing else for *its* existence? In other words, "parts" of the world may depend on other "parts"; but may not the sum-total of all the parts be a self-existent whole?

Now we cannot go into the logic of this popular mode of thought further than to ask, "When and where is the world as a whole?" In other words, the whole-parts analogy will not do when one is talking about the world. The world is not a sum-total of things and events. And even if it were, the sum-total of *de*pendent things and events could not be an *in*dependent entity. Perhaps those who affirm that it could be are simply saying that *something* must be "taken for granted" as existing independently of all else, and that their name for this is "world" or "nature," while others say it is God who is Alpha and Omega, the self-existent. Is the argument then simply a matter of words?

Before answering this question, let us return to one

which has in a sense been bypassed in our reflections thus far: *Can* one think of self-existence—something which depends on nothing else for its existence; and is it necessary to do so? Some Christian theologians, like St Anselm, Archbishop of Canterbury in the eleventh century, have maintained that man can and must think of that which is greater than anything else conceivable, and that his very ability to do so proves that there *is* a self-existent, perfect being: God. St. Anselm's argument is called "the ontological argument" for the existence of God. This argument in effect says that if God did not exist man could never have thought of him—or rather, that man *must* think of him, and therefore he must exist. Every man, said Anselm, knows the meaning of the phrase "that than which nothing greater can be conceived"; the notion of an "ultimate" is a "given" of human experience. But if man can understand "that than which nothing greater can be conceived," then "that" must exist. Otherwise one might think of something which is "greater" because it exists in fact as well as in thought. A *non*-existing "that than which nothing greater can be conceived" is, in effect, a contradiction in terms. Man can and must *think* of perfect existence only because there *is* perfect existence; and this is God.

One who hears Anselm's argument for the first time immediately suspects that some kind of trick is being played. Perhaps, one thinks, there is a sense in which one understands the meaning of the phrase, "that than which nothing greater can be conceived"; but does understanding the meaning of the phrase really imply that the being intended by the phrase "exists"? This is precisely the question which Anselm's philosophical opponents have raised, from Gaunilon in the eleventh century to Immanuel Kant in the eighteenth century. To be able to think of anything surely does not mean that what we are thinking of must exist. One can think of all sorts of things which do not exist. Who said that "existence" is a *predicate*, anyway? And by what right does one assume that existence as a predicate is a necessary ingredient of "perfection," or "that than which nothing greater. . ."? One can think of a perfect island somewhere. In his imagination the island has all the features required by his notion of perfection. But whether there *is* such an island could only be decided by sailing the seas to find out. Or, as Kant suggested, one can think of a hundred dollars in his pocket. In his imagination these dollars have all the characteristics of coin of the realm. But, unfortunately, the only way one can tell whether there "really are" a hundred dollars in one's pocket is to stick in one's hand and "see." And no one has discovered "that than which nothing greater can be conceived" by exploration or by sensory contact.

Now defenders of Anselm would maintain that it is *only* with respect to God that it may be said that idea implies existence. It is true of everything else—that is, "everything *in* the world—and 'the world' as the 'sum-total' of everything 'in' it—" that existence can be known only on the basis of sensory contact. God is the only exception to this rule, and he is the one *necessary* exception. Things whose existence can be proved only by sensory contact are obviously not self-existing. Yet there must be *something* which is taken for granted as self-existing. Or, to put it another way, there must be some point at which thought and being coincide, by definition. This point is God. We cannot know God by sensory contact, yet our very ability to think of him—indeed, the *neces-*

sity of thinking of him—proves that he exists. If we said that the existence of God could be established only in the way in which the existence of things which are not God is established, then it would not really be God that we were talking about.

So we are back to the question whether "self-existence" is a meaningful concept, and whether the reality of a self-existent being can be established, if it cannot be established by the means usually employed to establish the existence of anything else. St. Thomas Aquinas, in the thirteenth century, reflecting on Anselm's argument, observed that if man could know God as he is "in his essence," then he would indeed know him as self-existent. *If* God is, he is self-existent. He is "that than which nothing greater in existence can be conceived"—dependent on nothing else for his existence. But St. Thomas noted that man, who seeks to know God, is *not* self-existent. He is finite rather than infinite, a creature rather than creator. He knows things as a finite being, and the things he knows are themselves finite beings. The finite cannot comprehend the infinite; man cannot "know" "that than which nothing greater..." because he is man and not God. If he *could* know it—or him as he is in himself—then by definition he would know it or him as self-existent. But, as philosophers and scientists have pointed out from the time of Aristotle, Aquinas' philosophical hero, to contemporary positivists, finite man can know things only on the basis of contact with them; and the things he can contact with his senses, are, like himself, finite.

Yet Aquinas did not conclude from this that the existence of God cannot be proved. It cannot be proved in the manner suggested by Anselm, he said, but there are other ways. Indeed, he said, there are *five* ways in which one may argue for the existence of God as a necessary implicate of the existence of the world. The five ways suggested by Thomas have, with modifications suitable to changes in man's scientific knowledge, been widely used by Christian philosophers since his time. It will be worthwhile to examine them briefly, then, in continuing our examination of the question whether God's existence can be proved.

In Thomas' first proof of the existence of God, he notes the existence of motion in the world. In the Aristotelian physics of his day motion was understood to be transition from a state of potentiality to a state of actuality. Things were thought to move because they were attracted by other things. Aristotle had said that, while any specific motion in the world might be understood in terms of the attraction of a specific actual state for a potential state, the total process of motion in the world—that is, the fact that there are actual states attracting potential states— could be accounted for only by an "unmoved mover," a state of pure actuality which is not itself in motion but is the final source of all motion in the world. There must be, as it were, a cosmic center of magnetism to account for the total network of magnetic motions. This *pure actuality*, the source of all motion, said Aristotle and Thomas, is God.

But this first of the five Thomistic arguments for the existence of God may leave the modern reader as unmoved as the unmoved mover. In modern physics, it would seem, there is no mystery about motion—and anyway, it is *rest* rather than motion which, if anything, needs further explanation. Is it not better simply to accept the fact that there *is* motion in the world, and work out such laws of its behavior as observation may warrant? The defender of Thomas' argument might reply that it is indeed true that for physics, or for any scientific system of explanation, there is no need to have recourse to such alleged entities as unmoved movers. But *physical* explanations leave unanswered *meta*-physical questions, and the theory of the unmoved mover is meta-physical—that is, it literally comes "after physics." It is an attempt to answer a question of an order which science need not consider, but which is a legitimate question for human inquiry in its wholeness. There are, in other words, always more why's to be asked after science has provided its explanations, and meta-physics provides non-scientific answers to some of these non-scientific questions.

This observation leads us to ask again what we do when we explain something scientifically. In popular language we would probably say that we have explained something scientifically when we have shown its "cause." Scientists themselves may not actually use the word "cause," but laymen generally assume that scientists are seeking the causes of things. And this leads us to ask what we mean by "cause." Aristotle noted that in the language of his day people meant four different things by this word; in assigning "causes" to things they were giving one or more of four different "rationales" of the things "explained." They might be showing what things or events normally precede the appearance of the thing or event in question. We would say that we explain *b* by noting that it is preceded by *a*; and *c* by *b*, and so on. To say that *a* is the cause of *b* is to say that when *a* occurs, *b* follows. We "explain" things by showing how they fit into sequences of events. In the light of proper observation, we can predict their occurrence. Scientific "laws" are, in this theory of "cause," statistical averages of how things usually happen.

But people also mean other things by "cause." In order to explain something scientifically, we say, we need not only to locate it in a sequence of events, but also to *define* it; to give its "form" in a "formula." That is, we must locate it precisely in a precise language-system, such as that of mathematics. Also, Aristotle said people sometimes use the word "cause" to tell what they think a thing is "for"—what its "purpose" is. If the acorn is the "cause" of the oak in the sense that the planting of acorns must precede the appearance of oaks, there is another sense in which the oak is the "cause" of the acorn as the goal of the processes of growth which lead to a full-grown oak. In living things there seem to be built-in patterns of purpose toward which the life-process of each thing moves. Striking instances of this have been uncovered in recent years by biologists and botanists. Indeed, workers in these fields are divided between "mechanists" and "vitalists," the latter maintaining that something like purpose in living things must be assumed in order fully to account for their observed behavior. But again we must note that the questions metaphysicians and theologians are interested in are not scientific questions. Regardless of which scientific theory may prove most useful to some people in accounting for some facts scientifically, there remains the fact of movement-toward-ends, and the use of the word "cause" to indicate what things are "for", or what their "use" is.

Then there is one more sense of the word "cause" which Aristotle noted in the linguistic usage of his day, and which also occurs in ours. People say they have "explained" the "cause" of something, when they have told what it is "made of"—what its "material" is. People today might say that in a very loose sense scientists "explain" water by showing that it is "made of " hydrogen and oxygen, and explain these by breaking them down into their atomic components, and so on. Things are explained, in other words, when they are shown to be specific configurations of matter or energy, which themselves are taken to be constant.

While this talk about what we mean by "cause" may seem beside the point, it is actually necessary because the average reader may not have realized that he means many different things by the word. Thus in asking whether it is necessary to appeal to God in order to explain the world, or whether the existence of God can be proved in the way the existence of other things is proved, in terms of causal connections, we are actually asking several *different* questions, which need to be sorted out. This is precisely what Thomas Aquinas attempted to do —to sort out uses of the word "cause," and to show that pursuing any question about causes far enough leads to recognition of the existence of God.

A specific event in the world might be explained causally, in any one of the four senses of "cause," by its relation to other specific events in the world. But *why is the world as such causally ordered?* Granted that things can be explained by reference to causality, *why is there causality?* The fact of causality itself, Thomas said, needs to be explained. And it seems more reasonable to extend the concept of "cause" in answering the question "why is there causality?" than to say that causality is the result of non-causal forces, or that it "just is." The fact of causality in the world, in other words, must be grounded in and explained by a "First Cause." Again we must note that a First Cause is not necessary for *scientific* explanations of things and events; rather it is an explanation of the fact that the world is such that scientific explanations are possible. And First Cause, said Thomas, is one of the things men have meant by "God."

The existence of God, then, may be proved by noting the facts of motion, and of causality in general, and proceeding to the answers necessary to account for the existence of these features of the world. A third way to argue for the existence of God, said Thomas, is to note the *contingency* of all things in the world. That is, nothing in the world exists necessarily; of anything in the world it might be said that "it didn't *have* to be." The world might just as well have been otherwise. Things come into being and pass out of being, and nothing endures or exists necessarily—or necessarily exists. And yet it is impossible that it should be true of literally *everything* that its existence is "contingent"—passingly dependent on the existence of other things, which are in turn passingly dependent . . . and so on. If this were the case then it would be possible for "nothing" to be—for there to have been a time, as it were, when nothing was. But this is impossible: out of nothing, nothing comes. Something cannot come out of nothing. Therefore, something must always "have been," and always "be," as the source of all that is. And that something must exist necessarily, dependent on nothing other than itself for its existence, or else it could not be the source of all that is. Necessary existence is also what men have meant by "God," said Thomas. He is The First and The Last—the creator and sustainer of all that is.

Fourthly, Thomas invites the inquirer to consider man's experience of degrees of perfection in the world.

Given in one's experience of things is their approximation, or lack of approximation, to a "perfect" case of the things in question. Men experience trees and sunsets and beautiful women. But a feature of the experience of these things is a sense of the *im*perfection of the most perfect instances of them one can think of. This sense of *lack*, it might be said, is at the heart of the aesthetic impulse and of man's drive toward creation of more perfect forms. Man, said Walter Pater, yearns for a "light that never was on sea or land." How is one to account for this immediately given sense of "not-quiteness" or "not-yet-ness?" Only in terms of the existence of a most perfect being, God, said Thomas. The perfection of God is seen refracted over the creation which is his handiwork, and pre-eminently in the mystery of man, who is his "image" or reflection.

Now the reader may be thinking that in these last two arguments Thomas has fallen back into a fallacy for which he criticized Anselm and others; that is, that he has argued from the necessity of *ideas* of necessary existence and perfection to the *existence* of a necessary and most perfect being. But Thomas and his followers would maintain that this is not the case. He does not begin with an idea, but with man's concrete *experience* of the world of which he is a part. He then notes certain features of that experience which are as "real" as the features of simple location in space and time revealed through sensory contact. The features to which he calls attention are those which concern poets and artists more than scientists; but they are none the less real features of the real world of human experience. He then goes on to ask how these features are to be accounted for, and shows that they may best be accounted for by the existence of a perfect being, God. The existence of God, in other words, is proved as a logical inference from publicly available human experience.

Finally, Thomas turns to the fourth of the senses of the word "cause" examined above, and notes the pervasiveness of *order* and *purpose* in the world. Things occur, not haphazardly, but in patterns. The more we learn about the inner workings of nature the more we are amazed by the intricate arrangements and balances of all things, from the smallest particles of matter to the vast reaches of the heavens. As we contemplate an amoeba or the Milky Way, we instinctively ask, "Could all of this have 'just happened'? Is it all a matter of 'chance'?" When we consider what happens in that segment of the world which is open to human experience and control when we "leave things to chance" or randomness, it seems impossible that all the order in the world could be the result of chance. We see design and purpose in things; there must be, therefore, a cosmic designer or purposer. Again we must note that such a concept is not necessary for scientific explanations. But to many, like Thomas, it seems the most reasonable and logical way of talking about the fact of order which science continuously reveals.

Here, then, are some major lines of argument which some philosophers and theologians have followed in their efforts to prove the existence of God. What are we to make of them? One objection to them which might immediately be raised is that they are attempts to deal with matters beyond man's capacities. The "explanations" they offer, it is said, are all *too* human! The eighteenth-century philosopher David Hume, in his famous *Dialogues on Natural Religion,* pressed this point relentlessly.

Even if we granted, for instance, that in human experience there are instances of something like order or purpose, by what right do we transfer these characteristics to the world as a whole, of which we have really so little and such imperfect knowledge? By what right do we say that the world as a whole—which, of course, we never actually *experience*—is "more like" one of its parts than another, or is characterized by one of its features any more truly than it is characterized by other features? And what is added to man's knowledge of the world when it is said that, in addition to specifiable causes of specifiable effects, there is a First Cause of all causes? The world is the same world, with or without a First Cause. If a First Cause is unnecessary for scientific explanation, is it not better to eschew any talk about such an entity? Can man really think of such a thing, or know what he is talking about when he talks about such a thing? And isn't the God whose existence is presumably proved by the arguments really too *human* to be God, too "anthropomorphic"? Doesn't he sound too much like a Superman, or a Big Producer, or a Master Designer?

This last question is indeed a crucial one for all theological discourse. At this point we can only pause to note that *all* language about *anything* is human language, and all human thought-systems are, in the last analysis, "anthropomorphic." In the age of relativity we are surely aware of the fact that we see things as men, from human viewpoints, and not as some other creatures occupying other viewpoints. In scientific language we seek to eliminate as much of the human and the relative as possible. The perfect language for science—mathematics—is indeed abstract and, in a sense, "unhuman." Someone has observed that you can say something mathematically about everything, but not much about anything. Why must it be assumed that the pale abstractions of mathematics speak more eloquently of what the world "*really* is" than do the rich metaphors of the poets? A First Cause or Necessary Being is not a mathematical entity, to be sure; but he may be as truly necessary for a truly human understanding of the world as is the formula $e=mc^2$. Or, conversely, it might be remembered that mathematics is also a human creation. Indeed, man's science may be his supreme poetic achievement. The point is that there is no good reason why one kind of human concern and human language should claim a privileged status over all others. It is important to know what kinds of questions one is talking about when he uses a specific kind of language, and not to get one's questions and languages confused.

Immanuel Kant saw the point of some of Hume's criticisms; indeed, he said that Hume's questions "aroused him from his dogmatic slumbers." Kant's response was to re-examine man's ways of knowing things through "pure" or scientific reason, in order to see what if anything may be known about the world and God in this way and thereby to "make room for faith"—or, to use Kant's language, to make a more precise distinction between arguments from "pure" reason and arguments from "practical" reason—the rationale of *praxis*, the practical, decision-filled moral existence of man. Kant agreed with Hume that God is not an object of sensory experience. But neither is the self or the world, said Kant. We can never put our fingers on ourselves; we can never point to "I". We can only put our fingers on various objective or behavioral evidences of *me*, as an object among other objects in the world. Science knows objects, not subjects. Similarly, "the world" is never experienced as an object. The evidence of the world is never finally in, and we could not comprehend it if it were. "Self" and "world," said Kant, are "regulative ideals"—they represent necessary organizing principles of knowledge, but they are not themselves objects of scientific knowledge.

The same is the case with God. It is necessary, said Kant, to ground the self and the world in a common "object" which transcends both, or else we could never know that anything known by a self was true of the world which is not the self. St. Anselm had seen this, in his ontological argument for the existence of God. But St. Anselm had erred in thinking that what he had proved was an *existent*: he had only proved the intelligibility or necessity of the *idea* of God. Is there, then, any way in which the *existence* of God may be proved? Kant thought there is, but he thought that its point of departure is man's experience of moral values and moral law rather than his experience of facts and natural law.

First Kant had to show that there is such a thing as moral law. And this cannot be shown, he said, on the basis of man's experience of what *is* the case in any human situation—that is, moral law is not an implicate of any facts. The only thing that science, which deals with facts, can tell us about conduct is (a) how men actually do behave in various circumstances and (b) what means are likely to be the best ones to employ if men wish to change their behavior to achieve other goals, or conform to other ideals. But which goals men *should* seek, or which ideals they should honor, cannot be known simply from an analysis of what they actually *do*. Is there any law of value experience which should apply always and everywhere? Not if you try to find it by nose-counting or cultural analysis; "mores" are relative to cultures. But a rational examination of what is presupposed in all moral judgment—that is, in the principles of criticism of mores—reveals one, and only one, moral law, said Kant. It is that one should never make an exception of himself in making moral judgments. This is the principle of "equality before the law"—that is, the moral law. In no other sense are men equal. And if men are equal before the moral law, then one ought always to treat people as ends and not as means.

But what has this to do with the existence of God? The fact that men do and must recognize the moral law, said Kant, is not finally intelligible unless there is a God who is the giver and guarantor of the moral law. There is a "given-ness" about moral law which testifies to a law-giver. Moral law demands an obedience which goes beyond any and all factual considerations, and any and all "natural" or scientific explanations of its existence. Only by reference to God can man's denial of or victory over "the world" in the service of morality be accounted for. The supreme good for man is not happiness, but worthi-ness—worthiness to be happy. And yet happiness is also a good. In a truly rational world there must be, some time and somewhere, a harmony of worth and happiness. In other words, there must be immortality, a condition in which man can continue to approximate the moral ideal he can only partially approximate under conditions of space and time, and in which happiness will be related to worth in a manner which is notoriously not the case in earthly life. But immortality would be meaningful only if there were a divine harmonizer of worth and happi-ness—in other words, an existing God who is Judge and Redeemer.

Our summary, of course, does not do justice to Kant's argument, but perhaps enough of his intention is evident to see that he was attempting to put argument for the existence of God on another footing. He wanted to start from the distinctively human, subjective experience of value rather than the scientific experience of fact. Many theologians since his time have followed his lead, and have presented various popular variations of Kant's argument, sometimes stressing value experiences other than or in addition to those of moral value.

But many would feel that Hume's basic questions remain unanswered by the Kantian shift of argument. Is the God of Kantian proof any more clearly an existent than the God of the older proofs from "facts"? At most has Kant shown anything more than the intelligibility of the *idea* of God as moral ground and guarantor? Does not Kant's criticism of Anselm apply equally to Kant? And has Kant really proved that there is a moral law to be accounted for? Or, if he has, may it not be accounted for as well in naturalistic as in theistic views of the world? If there is a moral law, why not just note it and try to act accordingly? What is added when it is said that the moral law is given and upheld by God? These are some of the questions which philosophers have raised with respect to Kant's argument and its various subsequent formulations.

There is a more fundamental religious issue involved in Hume's criticisms. We have noted that at the end of each of his arguments Thomas asserts: "and this is God"; or "this is what men have commonly meant by God." By what right does he do this? Is he reporting a fact of usage, or is he making a judgment of faith? If he is doing the latter, is it the personal, living, willing, judging-redeeming God of the Bible who is equated with the unmoved mover, First Cause, cosmic designer, and all the rest? The import of this question has probably already occurred to readers who have found themselves saying, if they had the patience to follow the arguments—and whether or not they were convinced by them—"But this is not a God to whom I could say my prayers. This may be the God of philosophy," they would say, "but this is not the God of living religion. Philosophers seem to quarrel among themselves as to whether the arguments are valid, and as to what, if anything, they prove. If they do prove that there is a First Cause or Lawgiver—well, that's that. But whether they do or not, the life of religion will go on, and people will continue to argue about it."

This remark leads us to ask again, "What *is* 'the life of religion'?" There may be a sense in which Anselm's, Thomas', and Kant's arguments, and subsequent refinements of them found in theological textbooks or presented in popular form from pulpits and platforms, do call attention to that which is at the heart of the life of religion: namely, a sense of mystery, awe, and wonder. Thomas and the others may be saying, "take hold of the world wherever you will, and pursue the question 'why' just a few steps, and you wind up in mystery." The sense of mystery is increased rather than dissipated by increases in scientific understanding of the world. Poets and other artists constantly call attention to the mystery and the miracle of the commonplace. Perhaps philosophical theologians like Thomas, in a more ponderous and technical fashion, are systematically exhibiting the mystery of the world. There are philosophical as well as liturgical ways of expressing a sense of the holy. Certainly Kant had a profound sense of the holiness of moral obligation.

It is worth noting that when Thomas had finished his monumental volumes of theology, he placed them on an altar and called them an "unworthy sacrifice." Whether one "touches bottom" in his thinking through analysis of his immediate selfhood, or reaches out to the limits of man's knowledge through consideration of features of the objective world, he comes ultimately to limit-questions. These are perhaps the most difficult; possibly the most profound; and surely the most human and important questions one can ask. One's final response to them is his religious faith, whatever that response may be. Christianity is a way of living out answers to such ultimate questions. And we have seen that at the heart of the Christian response is, not a philosophical theory, but a Person.

V

"Of course when Christians are pressed on any of these matters they always say it's a 'matter of faith.' What is that? How can an honest person say he believes something that can't be proved, or that he knows isn't so? ... (Augustine: a case-study in faith and reason). . . How could you square the existence of a good God with the existence of so much suffering and evil in the world?."

"Of course when Christians are pressed on any of these matters they always say it's a 'matter of faith.' What is that? How can an honest person say he believes something that can't be proved, or that he knows isn't so?"

It is true that Christianity is a "matter of faith." It is more accurate to speak of the Christian faith than to speak of the Christian philosophy or the Christian theory of life. Christianity, like other religions, constitutes a way of living as well as a way of believing, and it involves one's *practice* in all the details of life as well as one's *theory* as to what it's all about. Like other religions, it is uniquely rooted and expressed in the life of worship as distinctively religious activity. But when one says that Christianity is a "matter of faith" it is well to be as clear as possible as to what one means by the term "faith"; and our interlocutor's question indicates that both Christians and their critics are frequently far from clear on the matter.

Many Christians use the word "faith" in such a way as

to suggest that for them it is indeed a matter of "believing—or pretending to believe—something one knows isn't so." The average Christian feels very uncomfortable when he is asked too many questions about the basis of his professed belief. He probably has not thought very much about it, and certainly has thought less critically and maturely about it than he has about many other things in his life. So, when he is asked why he believes what he believes, he is likely to fall back on an emotional glow carried over from childhood experiences at home or in church, and call that glow "faith." He *feels*, he says, that the Christian faith is true, but he "can't explain why." It may be that he even feels that attempts to explain why are somehow impious: signs of lack of faith.

There are, on the other hand, some things he thinks he knows, such as that two and two make four, or that the sun will rise tomorrow. He may even claim to "know" that "honesty is the best policy" or that "God helps those who help themselves." He knows some things about his daily work and about other people; but when he comes right down to it, he doesn't think he knows very much about "God and religion and all that sort of thing." Indeed, some of the things he says he "believes" when he recites a creed, for instance, he *does* know "not to be so" in the literal sense in which he understands the words of the creed. If he understands the word "God" to mean, vaguely, an abstract principle of explanation of the world, then surely he must know that such a God could not be "made flesh" in a man. Or if he turns to science to provide models for what he usually means by "explanation," then he must know that it is scientifically nonsensical or irrelevant to talk about "God the Father almighty, maker of heaven and earth."

Science does not need a doctrine of creation. It simply assumes certain constants, and explains one thing by showing its relation to others in terms of these constants. So some Christians may find, when they press the matter far enough, that they really do use the word "faith" to affirm things they "know aren't so" in a certain sense of "know," and assuming certain meanings of the things affirmed. When they say of something that "it's a matter of faith" they may be saying, "Please don't ask any more questions about this; I find them embarrassing."

Yet the embarrassment of the Christian who uses the word "faith" as a way of covering up his embarrassment may be honest and salutary, and it may be an expression of something more profound than his questioner realizes. Note that the questioner himself uses the words "faith," "believe in," "know," and "prove" quite loosely. He assumes that faith and knowledge are mutually exclusive, when he speaks of faith as "believing something one knows isn't so." If this were the case, then to make a claim to know something "on faith" would be simply to make a false claim to knowledge. Then there are those other terms: "belief," and "believing in," and "prove." Knowledge, apparently, is thought to be a matter of proof, while faith and belief are not: people are alleged to believe things that can't be proved.

This, in turn, raises the question of what one means by "proof." How one proves that two and two make four may seem fairly clear, and when one pursues the matter he may find that the proof consists of spelling out one's definitions of mathematical terms. Given certain definitions of numbers and their relations, it "follows by definition" that in the most commonly used arithmetical system two and two make four. But one may go on to say that this isn't all he means when he says he can prove that two and two make four. He can point to four fingers and count them and show you that two fingers alongside two other fingers are four fingers; the fingers are matters of sensory experience. The case is similar with respect to the sun's rising tomorrow; too many men have experienced too many sunrises over too long a period of time to make it seem unlikely that the performance will not be repeated tomorrow. But note that one doesn't say that two fingers added to two fingers are *likely* to be four fingers; they *are,* "by definition." Yet it is only in a very special sense that one can say that the sun will rise tomorrow by definition—that is, unless one defines the sun as that heavenly body of a certain size which always rises in the east at dawn, and must always if it is to be called the sun.

We seem, then, to have two different but closely related senses of the word "proof" on our hands. In one sense, proof is a matter of definition and can provide certainty by definition. In the other sense, proof is a matter of sensory experience and can provide only probabilities, ranging from very small to very large probabilities. And then there are "faith" and "belief," which are sometimes supposed to provide neither the certainty nor the probability of "proof," though some people claim that they do. It is no wonder that our interlocutor thinks the Christian must be either confused or dishonest when he talks about all the things he "believes in" or "takes on faith." But part of the confusion may lie with the interlocutor and his own fuzzy uses of the terms of his question. Perhaps the course of wisdom would lie in seeing just what the words "faith" and "belief" have meant in the historic Christian tradition, without prejudice.

In the Biblical tradition of early Christianity, faith had to do with personal relationships and historical events. The response of Israel to the exodus from Egypt was a formal act of faith in the liberating God of the exodus. The account of the exodus itself shows the faith of Moses to have been of paramount importance in the accomplishments of that event. Moses responded to the call of the Lord of history in an act of trust which gave him the courage to face Pharaoh and lead the people out of bondage. Yet, according to the Biblical account, the faith of Moses was not a "simple" faith: he is portrayed as struggling with God, with himself, and with the people on numerous occasions, from the moment of his call and throughout his life. After the formal act of faith which ratified the covenant at Sinai, binding the people to Jehovah, there were numerous instances of infidelity expressed in failure of nerve. It was because of one of these, when the people were afraid to possess the land which was promised, that they were required to spend forty years in the wilderness in order to raise up a tougher and more faithful generation. In the Biblical account of crucial events of Israel's past, then, faith is portrayed as fundamentally the *trust* by which the people are called to live. It is not "blind" or without any basis in their experience; rather it is an open-eyed response to events which occurred, and an underlying attitude toward all future events in the light of these. It is expressed in obedience to the God in whom they have put their trust. Disobedience of his law is taken to be symptomatic of lack of trust, or infidelity.

This is the great theme of faith which runs throughout the Old Testament: Israel is called, through events of national history, to trust in God, and her future actions are interpreted in the light of that trust or its breach. The prophets constantly charged Israel with faithlessness expressed in economic injustice, cowardly political and military action, and hypocritical religiosity. They frequently compared Israel's relation to God with the relation of husband to wife. Israel was Jehovah's "bride," they said; she had been chosen by him and had "pledged her troth." She had done nothing to win his favor, and he was faithful to her even in her unfaithfulness. Again and again Israel was called upon to "keep the faith" in the midst of calamitous historical events.

With this understanding of faith as the basis for community life, later Biblical writers could speak of faith in terms of inner, personal life. Prophets like Jeremiah portrayed their own inner struggles to keep the faith in the midst of misunderstanding and ridicule. And in the Book of Job one finds perhaps the supreme dramatization of the Old Testament understanding of faith. Rejecting all the formulas by which men had thought they could understand and control their relation to God, Job pours out his sense of God-forsakenness to the God beyond the God of the formulas. Through the courage of his despair he is brought to a closer and more profound communion with God, of whom he had previously "heard with his ears," but now finally "sees" in a new and more intimate relation. Job received no rational answers to the problems which tormented him; he gained a new attitude toward them which could sustain his despair and put the matter of answers in a secondary place.

This, then, is what faith in God meant to Jesus' people. It was not a matter of intellectual assent to a body of propositions, or a way of explaining the inexplicable. It was rather a matter of inner conviction and commitment, expressed in a way of life. Its chief expression was *courage*. Robert Frost has a character in the *Masque of Mercy* say that "courage is of the heart—by derivation." Faith, in the Biblical sense, is fundamentally "of the heart." One's faith is where one's heart is, said Jesus. Paul Tillich entitled a recent book on the varieties of faith, *The Courage To Be*. One's faith is his "answer" to the question " 'to be, or not to be'—and if 'to be'—why?"

The basic affirmation of faith for early Christians, we have noted, was the confession "Jesus is Lord." This affirmation, like the acts of faith of Jesus' people, was not "blind"; it was based on personal experiences of people with Jesus as a person. Part of that to which those who made the affirmation were responding was the faithfulness of Jesus himself, "even unto death." The calm courage of the figure in the gospels, as he goes about doing the will of his Father, was and is for Christians both an example and a challenge. Yet even Jesus' faith was not "simple" and unruffled. There was bloody sweat in Gethsemane, and there was a cry of God-for-sakenness from the cross. His faith, said the Christians, was victorious even then, and with the courage of forgiveness he accepted those who would destroy him. His victory was definitively attested in his resurrection. The faith of the first Christians was a response to all this—a personal commitment to a person in whom they had seen victory over life and death. Their response, in turn, transformed their lives and gave them courage to spread the good news, frequently in the face of persecution. On the basis of his faith Paul could affirm that no experience of life could "separate him from the love of God"; he had learned "in whatsoever state he was to be content." In "peril, tribulation, nakedness, and sword" Christians are, he said, "more than conquerors." The "powers of darkness" had done their worst to Jesus and he had overcome them in his death. Through his own "death and resurrection," Paul said, he *"lived"*—joyously and confidently—"yet not I, but Christ lives within me."

Here, then, is something of the flavor of what faith meant for New Testament Christianity. When the early Christians spoke of their faith they were speaking of a basic attitude created by something that had happened to them as they encountered Christ, either directly in the flesh or indirectly through hearing the gospel and participating in the sacraments. To speak of faith was to speak of crucial events of "inner history," which were in turn responses to events of "outer history." These events provided their clue for understanding *all* events of inner *and* outer history—past, present, and future. But their faith was never easy, and never settled. And the understanding it gave them did not provide neat explanations of all that went on in their lives or the life of the world about them. Instead, it provided a way of living confidently *in* and *with* these events, explained or unexplained. "Faith," said Paul in a famous definition, "is the substance of things hoped for, the evidence of things not seen." Hope springs from a basic act of courage turned toward the future, and the "substance" of hope is faith. "Explanations" may be derived from careful analysis of "things seen"; but there are other realities in life which are "not seen." One's faith rests on the "evidence" of these—and *what* his faith is, is evi*denced* by the quality of his life.

We have seen that many faiths competed for men's

allegiance in the world into which Christianity came. Stoics, Epicureans, devotees of mystery-religions, worshippers of Caesar and the state, and many others offered formulas for the "courage to be." For many Romans the "pious Æneas" of Vergil's *Æneid* would be the example *par excellence* of the devoted man—or the man of faith. Piety has been defined as "loyalty to the sources of one's being." Vergil's picture of Æneas leaving burning Troy—carrying his father and the household gods on his shoulders, and with his son at his side—would be for many Romans, as for many moderns, a perfect picture of piety. Many people today would hold that one's family and one's nation are the sources of one's being, and that loyalty to them is the fundamental expression of faith. In this faith Æneas went forth to found Rome, the new Troy. For this faith many moderns would give their lives —for "a better deal for the kids." If asked *why* "a better deal for the kids" is a good thing, they would think the question irrelevant. It seems "self-evidently" good. In other words, it's a matter of faith!

Among those who heard the Christians proclaim their loyalty to Christ as in a very real sense the "source of their being," were some whose basic faith was in the courageous pursuit of free inquiry. The example *par excellence* of this faith was Socrates, dramatized and extolled by the philosopher Plato. Socrates' relentless quest for clear thinking, and for honest admission of ignorance on the part of his hearers and himself, resulted in his death. But in his way of taking his death, faith in honest inquiry triumphed over the ignorance and envy which always seek to throttle it, Plato said. Plato himself carried on the Socratic quest for knowledge—for something one could be *certain* of, and for clearly understood principles by which one could live. Increasingly, Plato saw the model of such certainty in mathematical knowledge. If only men could define moral principles as they can define mathematical "forms"! Plato's quest was in turn taken up by others who sought for rational explanations of man and nature, hopefully through one basic "idea" or "form" which could be the explanation of all else. All explanations of all events, said the Neo-Platonists, point toward and are grounded in one "form" of complete abstraction and absolute simplicity—called simply "The One."

Many men who were primarily motivated by this scientific-philosophical quest for understanding found their way into the Christian faith. The problem of the church, then—and in a sense the basic problem of all subsequent Christian theology—was to relate the Hebraic-New Testament understanding of faith as personal trust based on inner conviction and commitment, to the pursuit of wisdom and understanding extolled in Greek philosophy. In these latter, as in many modern views, the word "God," if used, would stand for a unified *explanation* of man and nature, based on the dictates and requirements of reason. For the Hebraic Christian the word "God" would stand for a more intimate and personal object—or, more accurately, *Subject* of that fundamental trust and commitment, in terms of which life in all its ambiguities and vicissitudes might be lived—and death, the final enigma of life, confidently faced. Can the human concerns clustered around the personal God of the Hebraic Christians be combined with the concerns expressed in the impersonal God of the philosophers? Can the life of faith in the Hebraic sense be combined with the life of reason in the Greek sense? What *is* the relation of Christian faith to the questions posed by the various attempts to prove the existence of God? This continues to be a question of crucial importance for Christians, and it is perhaps the question which the interlocutor to whom we are addressing these comments is really asking. Perhaps no one in the history of Christian thought asked this question more insistently, or answered it more powerfully, than St. Augustine of the fourth and fifth centuries. It would be worth while, therefore, to attend briefly to the gist of what he had to say.

(Augustine: A case-study in faith and reason)

Augustine was born in 354 in Tagaste, in what is today Algeria. His mother, Monica, was a Christian, and his father, Patricius, was a pagan and a minor consular official. Dispute and disharmony characterized Augustine's early home life. We know this, and much else about his life—indeed more than we know about the depths of any other life of antiquity—because later he remembered it all before God in a book called the *Confessions*. It has been said that this book marks the discovery of the self in Western literature. The drama it unfolds is the drama of a tortured soul seeking and finding peace. It is written from a position of transparent honesty— from a time in the life of its author when he could afford to be honest with himself, and when he could honestly review his "remembrance of things past." It has been called the first example of "stream of consciousness" literature.

In the *Confessions* Augustine not only presents the facts of external and internal conflict during his chilhood and youth; he also probes their meaning with pene-

136

trating psychological and moral insight. For instance, he notes that schooling was forced upon him, and that he hated it. Those who forced it did so for questionable motives, to glorify themselves through their son. Yet that which he hated, and which was wrongly forced, turned out to be a great good. He learned, he said, to read what was written and to write what he wanted to say—a rare educational achievement! He became enamored of the Latin classics, and began to develop a thirst for knowledge. But at the age of sixteen he had to drop out of school and spend two years at home in relative idleness, because of family financial problems. During this period, he said, he allowed "the filth of concupiscence to cloud the springs of friendship." His life was one of aimless recklessness.

Finally, he was able to go to Carthage to resume his studies. There he developed an interest in the theater, and in considering it later he puzzled over the fascination of enacted tragedy. The study of Cicero led him to espouse Stoicism for a time, and then he turned to a form of religious dualism called Manicheanism. The doctrines of the Manichees are obscure, but they seem to have believed in the existence of two cosmic forces, good and evil, warring against each other. Victory of the good was promised those "in the know" about its nature. Yet the problem of the irrational in life—of pain and of evil—continued to torment Augustine. Meanwhile, his highly libidinous nature was expressing itself in physical lust, and to assuage this he took a common-law wife named Melania, who bore him a son called Adeodatus—"gift of God."

After training at Carthage Augustine returned home to Tagaste, where he opened a school. He achieved immediate fame and success as a teacher—but he says that he was farther than ever from inner peace. Finally his universe was shattered by the death of his closest friend. The experience of bereavement, classically described in the *Confessions,* left him naked in spirit. He tried prayer, but it brought no relief—because, he said, his dead friend was more real to him than the "phantasm he then called 'God.' " Leaving the painful scenes of home, he went to Rome. There he embraced systematic doubt and skepticism. He determined to believe in nothing of which he could not be sure; and he could be sure of nothing in which he had formerly believed. But eventually, by tracing his doubt to its base, he became aware of the fact that he could not doubt the existence of his doubting self—he could not doubt that he doubted! Yet the self which doubted did not have true, complete, or certain existence. It was finite; it had been cast into being and would be cast out of being. It was subject to limitation and error; surely it was not the author or ground of certainty! If not, from whence did the notion of certainty come? And how was it possible for the self to be aware of its finitude? Whence the notion of infinity, which is implied by the notion of finitude? The self, concluded Augustine, must be grounded in a reality which *truly exists* and which is infinite. Awareness of error and the quest for certainty must be a reflection of truly existing, though dimly perceived, Truth. Thus Augustine was led toward belief in the God of Neoplatonic philosophy: the truly existent One which (or Who) is the source of Truth. The writings of Plotinus especially seemed to provide the answers he had been looking for.

From Rome Augustine went on to Milan, to be professor of rhetoric in the university. There he also gained new fame and fortune. To further the latter he decided to send Melania home, in order that he might marry a girl of more advantageous social status. Meanwhile, he said, he could not think of spending a night alone. It was becoming painfully apparent to him that the one thing from which his newly embraced philosophical knowledge could not free him was himself. For him, sexual desire was the symbol of self-enslavement. In his life, concupiscence was the focal point of human bondage. He was not free to be himself in relation to others; always the urges of physical desire transformed others into potential means to ends, of either mastery or enslavement.

Meanwhile, he had been going to the Christian cathedral in Milan to hear the preaching of Bishop Ambrose, whose rhetoric he admired. Once before he had considered briefly the Christian faith of his mother, but it seemed to be a childish thing—and he was not at that time, he said, prepared to "become as a little child." But Ambrose had been a successful lawyer and orator before his conversion, and he was pressed rapidly into the administrative work of the church. On one occasion he and his flock withstood a seige by the army of the empress, who had embraced Arian Christianity. Perhaps there was more to the faith than he had suspected, Augustine began to think. When he heard that Victorianus, whose translation of Plotinus he admired, had become a Christian, he wondered even more if there might not be intellectual resources in the faith which he had missed. Then he heard the story of the conversion of St. Antony, a young man who, like Augustine, was rich in many talents. Antony, the story went, stopped outside a Christian church one day to hear and to scoff at what was going on inside. Instead he became entranced by the words of the gospel, and when he heard someone read Christ's command to the "rich young ruler," "Go, sell what thou hast, and give to the poor," Antony had immediately gone off to do just that. Augustine began to see that nothing less than an equally radical transformation of his personality, an equally radical act of renunciation—or crucifixion—could bring him the peace, the resurrection he sought.

But this insight served only to intensify his struggle, which still dramatized itself in terms of lust. His description of "turning in his chains," of "almost but not quite" breaking them, of the whispers of his "ancient mistresses," urging him to think of what would forever be unlawful if he broke the patterns of familiar selfhood —all this is without parallel in the literature of souls in conflict. Finally, under dramatic circumstances, the break came. He was with a friend in a garden, pouring out his inner torment. In order to weep without offense, he withdrew to a place of privacy. There he became aware of children's voices, chanting "take up and read." Being unable to think of any game in which children might sing these lines. he interperted the words as a sign to return to the volume of St. Paul he had been reading, and to read what his eyes first fell upon. He opened, and read: "not in chambering and wantonness . . . but put ye on the Lord Jesus Christ." Immediately, he says, his old self was crucified and a new self burst into life, free from the self-defeating pretensions and enslaving drives of the past.

He resigned his teaching post in order to return with his mother and a few close companions to the villa of a friend, there to work out the implications of what had happened to him. At Easter time he presented himself to Bishop Ambrose for Christian baptism. Then he wished nothing more than to return to his home in North Africa, there to spend the remainder of his life in ascetic retirement and study. But he was pressed into the service of the Church, first as priest and then as Bishop at Hippo. For the second thirty-five years of his life he served the Church as administrator, scholar, preacher, and pastor. When he died in 429 the Vandals were at the gates of the city of Hippo—but he had given men a vision of the "City of God" in relation to the "City of Man" which was to sustain them through the decline and fall of many empires.

The basic realities of the Augustinian vision are the self and God; and, of these two, the only truly "self-evident" is God. He is the eternal self-existent, "He Who Is," the creator and sustainer of all. Since all that is not God is his creation, and God is good, all creation is also good. But some reality is farther removed from the pure being which is God than is other reality, and the degrees of "becoming" and "being" are degrees also of evil and good. Pure evil would be pure non-being. Dis-ease is decay; evil "is" only in a parasitical way, as a deprivation of good. So far Augustine agreed with Plotinus. But in his personal struggle with lust, and in all men's rebellion against recognition of their finitude, Augustine saw another dimension of evil which he called "sin." Sin is not mere absence of good—it is positive assertion of evil. It is the willfull espousal of finite goods over against God, or the exaltation of finite goods to a status appropriate to God alone. It was primarily through wrestling with the reality of sin that Augustine came to see God as personal will. What man has to do with finally, he saw, is not only universal "Being" or "Truth." God for Augustine was also, and perhaps pre-eminently, a *personal* reality, standing over against and in support of the willing, doubting, rebelling, accepting human individual. Man's good, said Augustine, lies in bringing his *will* into harmony with the *will* of God, as well as in bringing his *mind* closer and closer to such comprehension of divine Truth as may be possible for a finite mind.

"Love God—and do as you please," he said. If one loves God, one loves one's neighbor as one's self. Then what one "pleases" is to do good for the neighbor. To love God is also to love knowledge, and to pursue rational inquiry wherever it may lead, because doubt itself is possible only if God exists. Yet Augustine discovered that he could not free himself from that self-love which is an attempt to play God. The good news for him was that God would do for him what he could not do for himself. Likewise, man could not, he said, "by taking thought *a*scend to God." The good news was also that God could and did *de*scend to man to meet man as a Man—as Truth in Person. In the response of the whole being to the love of God incarnate in Christ, one may find his final freedom, and a triumphant faith for living.

"I believe, in order that I may understand," said Augustine. He saw that all understanding rests on some belief; some standing-place; something taken for granted—or, more accurately, "taken *as* granted." It was only when he took as granted the good news of Christianity that he could finally understand himself and his world. For Augustine, then, faith and reason are not contradictory or mutually exclusive. Rather, understanding rests on faith, and faith generates the obligation to understand. One must believe in order to understand; but one must understand as critically and intelligently as he can that which faith enables him to see, if he is to be faithful to his calling as a Christian. This view of the relation of faith to reason is one which has commended itself to many thoughtful Christians from Augustine's day to ours.

"How could you square the existence of a good God with the existence of so much evil and suffering in the world?"

Perhaps it would be well to begin a comment on this question with a further request for definitions of terms. The "problem of evil" is a crucial problem for any religious faith or philosophy of life, and major differences between views of life center on their treatment of this issue. It is well, therefore, to be as clear as possible as to just what the problem is. Sometimes the question is posed in such a way as to make it unanswerable by definition. For instance, what is implied by "square" in the question asked above? Are we asking for a rational *explanation* of evil—an explanation which, in the last analysis, would deny that evil is really evil—would explain it away? Evil, at least in some of its dimensions, is irrational; or at least we usually mean by "evil" some events of life which "make no sense whatever." If this is what we mean by the term, then a request to make sense of that which by definition does *not* make sense would be odd indeed. Yet this is just what many of us do when we ask for "answers" to the problem of evil. We want to know how evil could be, and yet somehow not be *evil*.

There have been many, including some in the Christian tradition, who have sought to deal with the problem of evil in such a way as ultimately to explain away the fact of evil in the world. We have seen that St. Augustine was attracted by this approach. Following the Neoplatonists, he reasoned that if being is in a sense by definition good, then evil must be non-being, or nothing. The more truly it can be said of a thing that it *is*, the *better* that thing is. Evil is the absence of good, just as darkness is the absence of light. Only light, in this analogy, has being, or is real. Disease is the absence of health, and decay is the absence of growth. Darkness, disease, decay, pain—all these have only a parasitical sort of existence, if they can be said to have existence at all. Complete disease would be death, or non-being; complete decay would be dissolution. Applying the analogy to the "body politic," Augustine observed that "there must be honor even among thieves." That is, in order for any society to exist, even an evil or parasitical and destructive society, there must be some "health," reflected in "honor," in that society. No society can be based entirely on lies, just as no body can be wholly disease-ridden. The true society is the healthiest or most honorable society, just as the true man is the one who most completely lives the unique qualities of manhood. We say of one whom we admire that "he is a real person," and of one we do not admire that "he isn't much of a man."

There may be some merit in calling attention to this way of talking, at least in order to indicate that *there would be no problem of evil if there were no good in the world*. There is a sense in which evil exists only by negation or by default. But surely this is not the whole story! Pain is no less painful when we realize that it is the negation of pleasure. Or, even if it could somehow be shown that evil processes are parasitical, and can sustain no life of their own, there would remain the question as to why there should be these parasitical realities in the world. Why should there be darkness as well as light; suffering as well as health? Some who hold the view that evil is only the absence of good have said that the world is "better" with evil in it than it would be without it, because evil provides the contrasts and challenges necessary for appreciation of the good. Just as a painting cannot be all light if it is to be pleasing, but must have shadows and highlights, so life must have its valleys and shadows if the magnificence of its peaks is to be fully enjoyed. But—while it cannot be denied that only those who have known sickness can fully appreciate the blessing of health, it is doubtful that this reflection can be of much comfort to one who is suffering. Those who are in the shadows are no less in darkness when they are told that darkness is "merely" the absence of light. Furthermore, there seems to be no neat working out of the the light/darkness analogy for life. Many people seem to know little but darkness, and others seem to be mostly children of the sunshine. If the light/darkness analogy were to serve as an "explanation" of evil, then the picture of life as most of us know it would have to be judged ugly indeed!

Nevertheless, something in the human spirit seems to rebel against taking evil as a final reality. Many great religions, like Buddhism and Hinduism, have made the affirmation that evil is not "really" real, in the last analysis. Man's experience of what he calls evil, they say, is the result of his finitude—his ignorance and his limitations. If one could see all of reality from the aspect of eternity, as it were, then he would see that what men call evil is part of a total and necessary structure which is good—or, more accurately, is *beyond* such human appellations as "good" and "evil." Whatever happens in space and time, say Hindus and Buddhists, happens according to inexorable causal law (the "law of *karma*"). Just as one thing follows another in the realm of nature according to this law, so also men reap what they sow. But there is within man the capacity so to know and to co-operate with the laws of nature and of morality as to rise above their effects: to move toward that indifference to the necessary which is a reflection of Brahman, the "really real" for the Hindu—or toward that *detachment* which is the ideal of Buddhahood for some Buddhists.

In Western philosophy men like Spinoza of the sixteenth century have offered similar views. There is no good or evil "under the aspect of eternity," said Spinoza; things happen as they do because of natural law, and this lawfulness of reality extends to the psychological and moral dimensions of life. Only the ignorant man wants what he cannot have, or wants things like fame, pleasure, or riches, which do not last and cannot bring lasting joy. To know why things are as they are is to be serene in the experience of them. Knowledge is the one good that never lets you down. Spinoza commended to men, therefore, "the intellectual love of God": dedication to inquiry wherever it may lead, and a striving toward that "synoptic" vision of things in which the necessity of everything's being as it is can be understood. Deliverance from ignorance is deliverance from evil.

Again the average reader may respond to this line of reasoning with the feeling that there is much wisdom in it, but that it somehow does not fully come to grips with the problem of evil as he knows it. It is true that what men take to be evil frequently turns out "in the long run," or in the light of a "broader view of things," to be good. It is also true that much of the evil men experience is the result of their not knowing any better, and that the extension of knowledge in the world may result in the reduction of disease, conflict, pain and suffering. Yet there remains the question: "Why the *illusion* of evil—if it *is* in some sense illusory?" Why is it necessary to learn? Why is there ignorance to be overcome? Why do the wisest of men actually know so little, and why have most men in the world's history been doomed to lives of ignorance, and hence of frustration and evil? Is salvation, or deliverance from evil, only for the intellectuals: for those "in the *know*"? If so, how is one to account for all the rest in a presumably "good" world? More basically, there is the question whether serenity or blessedness *is* proportionate to knowledge. Is it true that men become better and happier as they come to know more? Some men have seen *less* rather than *more* sense in life as they have extended their experience and knowledge. We all see a measure of truth in the maxims "ignorance is bliss," and "what you don't know can't hurt you."

Maybe now we can see that "explanations" of evil which would "square" it with reason in such a way as to make the irrational "really" rational are bound, in the long run, to seem inadequate. This is because they are seeking to do that which is by definition impossible: to make the irrational reasonable, while at the same time affirming its irrationality. To say that evil is only "provisionally" irrational is to leave unanswered the question why the "provision" is necessary in a reasonable world.

Most of us need to give much more thought to what we mean by "evil" if we are to get anywhere in talking about the problem. In the preceding discussion we have lumped together under this term all sorts of things men don't like, from physical pain to frustrated desire. The first step in any fruitful consideration of the problem of evil is to start getting our evils sorted out. There is the apparently senseless pain and suffering of "nature red in tooth and claw," which is one feature of the struggle for survival. There are natural calamities like earthquakes and hurricanes, which seem to be given features of the same nature whose orderliness and benignity is otherwise so much admired. (One wonders, in passing, why it is *such* natural events rather than others that are frequently termed "acts of God"!) There is all the unfulfilled potential of wasted or thwarted human souls. And there is "man's inhumanity to man"—all the evil that man brings on himself by using his freedom and his talents to destroy rather than to create; to inflict pain rather than to bring healing. To deal with one of these kinds of evil in a way that may seem helpful is not necessarily to deal with the others. Conversely, such light as one may gain with respect to one of them should not be dimmed by his realization that there are unanswered questions with respect to others. In other words, it is neither "cricket" nor helpful to jump from one type of evil to another in arguing for or against views of the problem of evil in general—if there is any such thing as "evil in general." It is well to be as specific as possible about just what one is and is not talking about. The problem will not disappear with clarification, but a lot of talk about it may turn out to be talk about false issues.

Consider a further example of the fact that an alleged solution to the problem of evil in one of its dimensions may prove to be inadequate for dealing with other facts of life which men call evil. St. Paul and St. Augustine were forced to question the view that evil is merely a matter of ignorance. St. Paul discovered that the problem of making sense of his life was not simply a matter of *knowing* what he should do. He knew well enough, he said, what was needed to bring his life into harmony with the will of God—or, as others might put it, with the authentic or rational structure of being "as it really is." He was steeped in the Law. But through painful struggle he came to see that knowledge of the Law was not enough: "the good that I would, I do not; and that which I would not, I do. O wretched man that I am!. . ." Knowledge of the Law provided standards, but not the motivation or the ability to live up to them. Worse still, outward conformity to the Law could lead to that self-satisfaction and spiritual complacency or self-righteousness which is the very essence of sin.

Now part of the problem at stake here may turn again on definition—this time a definition of "knowledge." Those who would hold that "knowledge is virtue" may say that they include in the term, "knowledge," such insight as is necessary for motivation to do good, as well as theoretical understanding of what men should do. The knowledge which Plato urged men to acquire is *self*-knowledge as well as dispassionate vision of the standards or "forms" of nature and conduct. If this be the case, then St. Paul could go on to say that he came to know some things about himself through his encounter with the Risen Christ which literally made all the difference in the world to him—made a "new creature" of him. More accurately, he came to *accept* some things he had always known, but which he could not accept so long as he believed that he had to earn his salvation—had to prove his right to be accepted by God. It was only when he no longer had to pretend that he could drop his pretenses.

The experience of St. Augustine—and, we are of course suggesting, perhaps the experience of every man, in some guise or to some degree—was similar. Through strenuous pursuit of various philosophies and theologies he came to accept certain answers to the problem of evil in some of its aspects. At one point he thought the Manichees made sense when they said there are two great cosmic forces at work in the world, one good and one evil. Such a view seems at least to take evil seriously, and it has commended itself to many thoughtful men in various philosophical and religious traditions. If one can identify the two forces and their effects, then he can enlist in the service of the good and work toward triumph over evil. But how does one know that there will or can be a triumph? Some would say that one doesn't *need* to know; to fight for the good is good, no matter what. Yet what is one to make of the "total picture" of the world in which good and evil forces are at war with each other? Are good and evil two independent realities, or are they expressions of one reality which is basic to both? As he pursued these questions Augustine was led to affirm that evil is real, but only provisionally. It exists, but it can be overcome through the secret and "saving" knowledge provided by Manichaeism. (Some moderns might substitute the "saving knowledge" provided by science, or the knowledge possessed by those who are in the know about some philosophical, economic, or political formula or panacea.)

Life proved the inadequacy of this view for Augustine. A crucial experience, we recall, came with the death of his closest friend. It was all well and good to say that death was only the absence of life; or that in the light of the knowledge provided by his philosophy it could be said that his friend was not "really" dead and that the "real person" was immortal, while only the body died, in conformity with the general laws of decay. But the experience of bereavement—of the torturing absence of the one whose presence had given life part of its meaning —nevertheless left him with a sense of meaninglessness in life; grief gave the lie to the theoretical comforts of his philosophy. The dead friend was more real to him than the consolations of his faith—more real than "the phantasm which I then called 'God,'" he said.

If the experience of bereavement proved evil to be a more insistent reality than his philosophy could handle, his struggle with self-will expressed in lust revealed to Augustine an even deeper and more enigmatic dimension of the problem. Like Paul, he came to see that his knowledge could bring him freedom from ignorance and from much else that thwarted and soured life . . . but it could not bring him freedom from his last and worse enemy: himself. He too, knew what it was to "do that which he would not do." His account of his struggle to "break the chains" of his final slavery is a classic portrayal of a situation all too familiar to many of his readers. For his lust some might substitute alcohol, or popularity, or "being different," or political power, or family pride, or a thousand and one other symbols of self-justification. Augustine came to see that bondage to any or all of these may be symptomatic of man's fundamental reluctance to be who and what he is: to admit and to live with his finitude, in freedom; to pretend to have no *more* and no *less* virtue, or intelligence, or "personality" than he has. It was only when Augustine believed the good news of

151

man's acceptance by God proclaimed in and through Christ that he felt he was free, in principle, from himself —and free to be himself.

The experiences of Paul and Augustine are typical of those human experiences which lie at the heart of specifically Christian comments on the problem of evil. In the Biblical tradition from which Christianity comes, evil is primarily associated with man's inhumanity to man, and with the struggle of the Chosen People to be what they were called to be—to obey the law of God. At the personal and individual level, it is the problem of the individual's trust in God in the face of temptation. No philosophical or theoretical explanations of the fact that there is temptation are offered in the Bible. The myth of man's creation and fall in the Book of Genesis simply portrays in vivid and dramatic fashion the fact that "evil posits itself," and that man is responsible for himself and what he is, as a creature of God.

For a long time the Biblical people thought that if they lived up to their responsibilities by obeying the decrees of God, they could achieve goodness and would be rewarded with such suitable tokens of goodness as long life, prosperity, and security. Like the Hindus and Buddhists and all others who have reflected much on life, they observed that by and large men reap what they sow. But unlike others they soon saw that this is the case *only* "by and large." The Jewish nation suffered calamity after calamity, and there came a time when all of this could not be simply attributed to disobedience of the will of God. Or if it were, prophets like Ezekiel began to see that on this theory only a goodness sufficient to compensate for their evil could extricate the people from their tragic predicament. Were the people capable of this goodness? Or—and this is more significant for religious thought—did this mean that God was in a sense at the mercy of his people—that he *had* to punish and reward them according to a set formula? If so, who was really in control of the world? The prophet Hosea portrayed Jehovah as saying, "I am God and not man . . . and *therefore* I will forgive and redeem a wayward people who do not and cannot *deserve* forgiveness and redemption." God, said Hosea, is the one who is truly "free"—free to go beyond the requirements of justice alone. If he were not, then man's situation would be hopeless indeed! Ezekiel said that God would restore Israel in order to proclaim his *holiness*—his Godly power and transcendance; and then, *following* their unmerited deliverance, the people of Israel might repent and live in grateful obedience.

The most dramatic and suggestive comments on the problem of evil in the Old Testament are found in the Book of Job. This is a book of many meanings, whose dramatic power has challenged and inspired many artists from its own time to ours (see Robert Frost's *Masque of Reason* and Archibald Macleish's *J.B.*). At one level it is a probing rebuttal of the view that men always reap as they have sown. Job is presented as a man who is righteous by all the accepted standards of righteousness of his day and his people. Yet his family and his possessions are wiped out overnight, and he is reduced to physical torment and spiritual abandonment. The Tempter has posed the question: "Can a man be good—for *nothing*?" Is there such a thing as disinterested goodness? Job's problem is intensified when a committee of the orthodox call on him and attempt to comfort him with "answers" to his problem—the problem of the apparently unmerited suffering of the apparently righteous man. He *must* have done something to deserve his predicament, they say. Job had always held the view that men get their just deserts; let him now face up to applying the maxim to his own case. What man can claim that he is righteous before God? Is any man so sure of his goodness that he can say to God "You don't dare do this to *me*?" There was a lesson to be learned from his suffering, if Job would learn it; God wounds, but he binds up; the ordeal is intended for Job's good.

Most readers would perhaps recognize elements of truth in each of the "answers" offered by Job's friends. But Job turns on his friends and calls them fair-weather friends. He had expected more. He steadfastly maintains his integrity, demanding to be shown, by his friends or by God, where he has gone astray. He will not admit error of which he is not convinced; he will not stoop to hypocrisy. He has the courage of honest doubt. More important, his friends are in a sense offering answers to an unasked question. Job's predicament calls, not for theoretical analysis of the problem of evil, but for a sense of sustaining presence in a meaningless situation. Job has learned the difference between *thinking* about evil and *experiencing* it; the friends, apparently, have not. So he turns from them to God, and pours out his sense of God-forsakenness—to God. To whom else could he express his deepest despair? He rails against God; then he passes into moments of desperate hope; ("I know that my redeemer liveth. . ."); and then he sinks again into the depths of utter abandonment. He would welcome death, if only death would not simply seal off any possibility of meaning in his experience; if only he would not die forever misunderstood. He longs for God to show his pres-

154

ence in this ordeal which bespeaks only the absence of God.

Eventually God speaks—but in "the voice of the whirlwind." Job has been asking questions, says the voice; let him now answer a few. Can he explain creation? Where was he "when the morning stars sang together and the sons of God shouted for joy?" Does Job know the way of the sea; of the rain and snow; of horses and wild goats; of a thousand and one natural wonders? Surely he must know so much, to know that God is wrong and that life is meaningless because Job suffers! Job replies that he cannot answer. He has been talking when he should have been listening; he has been talking about matters beyond his depth from the beginning. More natural wonders are paraded before Job's eyes through the poetry from the whirlwind, and the sense of majesty and mystery intensifies until Job "repents, in dust and ashes."

Of what does Job repent? Of questioning God? Of being not only good, but too *sure* of his goodness? Of being not only righteous, but also self-righteous? There are those who have seen these "lessons" in the Book of Job. But Immanuel Kant, the eighteenth-century philosopher, held that Job's steadfast holding to his *integrity* to the bitter end is the chief greatness of Job. As the book ends Job is not rebuked by God for his doubt and his honest expression of abandonment. Rather, Job's orthodox friends are rejected by God because they had not spoken as truly of God as had Job. They had fallen into the blasphemy of thinking they had God in a box—had the ways of deity all wrapped up in neat formulas. The friends could be restored to grace only if Job would pray for them. Someone has suggested that this was the last, acid test of Job's goodness—that he must pray for "that committee"; for those who misunderstood him. Job prays, and the friends and Job alike are restored to knowledge of divine favor. Surely by now it must be obvious to the reader of the book, however, that the restoration to divine favor is not the effect of a cause. It is not a "reward" for one more act of goodness.

In the terms in which the problem of evil is usually put, Job receives no "answers." The mystery of suffering is no less mysterious after all is said and done in the book. But it is placed in the context of the mystery of life as such. Job receives no answers, but he receives something more important: a new *attitude* toward the problem which puts the matter of answers in its proper, secondary, place. Perhaps the problem of evil is, at the practical level of living, basically a problem of attitude or posture toward life, in the face of all the goods and bads, all the knowns and unknowns, with which life presents us.

Ivan Karamazov, in Dostoevsky's *The Brothers Karamazov*, thought so. He does not reject God, he says at one point in the book; he rejects the mess which is allegedly God's world. Could he "bless life," when life contained helpless babies suffering the effects of man's inhumanity to man? If he could not, then he would "respectfully hand back his ticket" and "take to the ways of the alley." Here is life, with its pain and its happiness, its wisdom and its stupidity, its greatness and its sham; on what terms is it to be lived? One may follow the advice of Job's wife to "curse God, and die." One may decide that it is better not to be than to be, if being is such a hellish mess. But if one decides to *be*, then on what *terms* will he be? Is there any *reason* for blessing life rather than cursing it? Can one have the honesty of his convictions and be consistent in actions which should follow from either attitude? Dostoevsky's readers are not told how Ivan finally resolves his dilemma; at the end of the book he seems to be undergoing an inner crucifixion, which may or may not lead to a resurrection.

But others in the book, and pre-eminently Alyosha, the brother Dostoevsky calls his hero, find a way of blessing life. Each of them undergoes a crucifixion of false securities and neat answers before the way is found— and the way that is found seems to lead *always* through a crucifixion, just as Job's way led him through despair. The way to bless life is not to ignore its evil or pretend it isn't there. Indeed, it may be that only one who has found a way to bless life can fully face up to the enigma of evil— that only those who don't have all the answers can live with evil. Mr. Antrobos, in Thornton Wilder's *By the Skin of Our Teeth,* returns from war against evil only to find its personification, his son Cain, lolling on the couch in his living room. "Ah Cain," he says, "it's so much easier to fight you than to live with you."

How *can* one "bless life" and yet live with the fact of evil? Returning to Dostoevsky, we note that Alyosha Karamazov found a way in seeking the *redemption* of the evil one, through patient and open acceptance. Alyosha was the brother with whom all could be honest, even in their evilness. And his non-condemning honesty was a more terrible judgment upon their evil than any other judgment could be. It was a judgment which could lead to the redemption of evil, because it reflected an honesty which *accepted* the evil one, as he was and in his contrition. Alyosha underwent his own crucifixion when the dead Elder of his monastery produced no miracles. Alyosha was disappointed again and again. But he was steadfast in his attitude of redemptive love. He had no answers to the problem of evil, but he had one way of *overcoming* evil!

Alyosha Karamazov may be taken as the Christ-figure of the novel. The conquest of evil through redemptive suffering is at the center of the Christian approach to the problem of evil. In the gospels Christ is portrayed as moving through life seeing it as it is and seeing men as they are, beneath the sham and pretense of either "goodness" or "badness" as popularly defined in the social mores of the day. His love is not a sentimental glossing over of sin; he has harsh words for the self-righteous, and he drives the money-changers out of the temple with a whip. He is not oblivious of the fact that towers fall on both righteous and unrighteous men. His Heavenly Father, he says, makes the sun shine and the rain fall on the just and the unjust alike. Wheat and tares grow together in the fields of human endeavor, and it is very difficult to tell one from the other . . . perhaps only God can, in the last analysis, or Last Judgment. But there is a last analysis and a Last Judgment—a truth about themselves by which men are finally judged and to which they are finally responsible. They may be led to accept that truth if they can be shown that the truth accepts them; that they are accepted by life—or by God—as they are, without pretense. They do not have to earn the right to be accepted; no man can. In Jesus' active and outgoing ministry of acceptance and reconciliation Christians have seen a way of living with evil redemptively. The final and most powerful act of Jesus' love, they say, was his death. On the cross he endured the worst that evil could do. The crucifixion, is, from one perspective, the ultimate tragedy of history. But Jesus' manner of dying, Christians believe, was attested by the resurrection to be the way of triumph over that which put him on the cross.

The problem of evil—as a "problem"—remains un-answered. But a way of blessing life has been found. "He is," says the Christian, "the way, the truth, and the life." Thus, when the Christian says that God exists and that he is good, in the face of the fact of evil in the world, he is not saying that there really is no evil, or that evil really is good. He is not saying that upon careful analysis it appears that the goods of life outweigh the evils; or that he knows that this is "the best of all possible worlds." Like everyone else, he knows only the ambiguous world that *is,* and he knows a way of blessing life in it. To say that God is good is to bless life; to bless life is to say that God is good.

VI

"Surely it won't do to say that it will all work out in an after-life, because immortality can't be proved either. . . . What would be the point of human effort if everything were in the hands of God anyway? . . . Christianity might make some sense as a private philosophy of life. . . . But who could ever think he had life all figured out?"

"Surely it won't do to say that it will all work out in an after-life, because immortality can't be proved either."

No, it won't do, though many people have tried to make it do. Job's friends tried to tell him that it would all turn out all right in the long run—though they did not include immortality in their view of the long run. Even so, Job saw the irrelevance of their "comfort" to the concrete fact of his suffering in the short run. And, if it were literally true that everything will turn out all right—is "bound to" or "has to" turn out all right—in the long run, then there is not much point in the short run. The short run would make no difference, in the long run. But if *today* makes no difference, life cannot be blessed today. And if life cannot be blessed today, it cannot be blessed.

The Biblical Hebrew progenitors of the Christians came late to any speculation about or belief in life after death. Moses, they said, "slept with his fathers," and so did David. God was where life was. He was the *living* God of Abraham, Isaac, and Jacob. If life was meaningful, it was meaningful in the concrete here-and-now of the daily grind or the daily joy; in a nation at war or enjoying peace; in a man enjoying the "delight of the law of the Lord," or crying from the depths of despair. Indeed, death was viewed by the Israelites as a separation from God, until finally they saw that if nothing in life could separate them from God, nothing in death could, either. If God had created Israel out of nothing, and had re-created her in deliverance from exile, then the creative-re-creative power of God could conquer death too: could raise up those whom God willed, to participate in the final triumph of his justice and mercy in history. They did not say that it *had* to work out all right in the long run, or that God *had* to raise up some to make it right. But if he were the faithful, redemptive God they had known in their turbulent history, he *might*: there were grounds for *hope*.

Christians said that the grounds for hope had become clearly evident—that there was fresh 'evidence of things not seen"—in the resurrection of Jesus. In that event the victory of redemptive love over all that would thwart it was most powerfully attested. Here was the basis for an abiding faith which produced an abiding hope expressed in abiding love, Paul said in 1 Corinthians 13. Faith is not knowledge, and hope is not certainty. Yet the uncertainty of hope is sufficient for blessing life. Indeed, said Paul, it is sufficient for the "persuasion" that "neither life nor death . . . nor any other creature" can separate the recipient of redemptive love from the source of redemptive love. All men live life in terms of one persuasion or another; this is the Christian persuasion. But note that in all of this there is no word about the immortality of the soul.

People who talk about the immortality of the soul have a view of man and God radically different from the Biblical-Christian view. There is something in man, they say, which is inherently deathless. At the primitive level they might speak of it as being like breath or wind, giving life and motion to bodies and passing on, but never dying out or dying down. Or it is like the "other self" which wanders out of the body in dream-states, or wanders into one's dreams or trance-visions from bodies long dead. In more sophisticated terms, others say that the immortal soul is that within man through which he grasps eternal truths and immortal "forms," and which therefore must itself be immortal. It is that which must be liberated from the "prison-house of the body," whose sensory experience and finitude is the source of error and deceit.

Over against this dualistic view of men the Bible portrays man as an indivisible unity, a creature made in the image of God "body and soul," but still a creature—by definition *mortal*. If there is more than mortality for man it must be "put on" or "added to" his mortality by the God who created him, said Paul. There is nothing in man inherently immoral; only God is inherently "from everlasting to everlasting." And, if there is more meaning in the presence of God than man can know this side of death, the body too must participate in that meaning on the other side. The body is not an impediment to be sloughed off; it is the temple of the spirit, the good creation of God. Thus the expression of Christian hope about death has from the beginning been in terms of "resurrection of the body. . ."

But as Christianity moved from a Hebraic to a Hellenistic world some Christian thinkers thought it was neces-

162

sary to express the Christian hope in the body-soul language of its host culture. Soon Christian theologians were talking about immortality, borrowing many of the arguments of the Platonists and others. Yet, as was the case with Augustine and Thomas Aquinas, they could never settle for these arguments as fully adequate expressions of the Christian hope. In the *Divine Comedy* Dante, dramatizing the theology of St. Thomas, has Vergil explain to the pilgrim through Hell that the souls there, or in Purgatory or bliss, await a more perfect experience of the state they chose for themselves while choice was possible—that is, while there was life, and thus hope. That more perfect state, of either bliss or torment, is *embodiment*. So much, he says, might be learned from Aristotle's philosophy as well as from Thomas' theological additions to that philosophy. Indeed, knowledge and practice of the four cardinal virtues of paganism might lead one to a pagan "limbo" of peace and light, of enjoyment of the arts and philosophical discussion, in the midst of the darkness and pain of Hell. There is, Dante says, only a *sighing* in that limbo—an awareness of an unimagined and thus unrealized good: the good of Christian love. That love can redeem men from sighing; indeed it once harrowed Hell to release those who had known it and lived by it even before it had become concrete in Christ. The movement of that love, said Dante, is from God-ward by grace. It came to the pilgrim of Dante's poem from the other side of his lostness in the Dark Wood of error and carelessness. "Reason," including so-called arguments for the so-called immortality of the soul, can at best lead men to a position where they might receive that which God offers but which they cannot achieve. Dante has perhaps expressed the Christian hope for life and death, and the Christian posture for blessing life, as powerfully as any artist in the Christian centuries. Those who do not know his poem may perhaps glimpse something of his meaning from these brief comments. But fully to know his meaning is to live in his poem, just as to know the meaning of the Christian hope about death is to live in that "poem" which is the Christian vision of life.

"What would be the point of human effort if everything were in the hands of God anyway?"

It does seem that the Christian really is saying that God is ultimately in control of things, and that he will bring matters to his own conclusion in his own time, whether people are around to witness that conclusion as immortal souls or resurrected bodies or not. And if this is the case, human effort in the interim does seem to be pointless. A popular Christian hymn says, "Rise up, O men of God, have done with lesser things!" Yet on the surface, at least, the Christian faith would seem to be saying, "Sit down, O men of God, there's nothing you can do!"

Perhaps it would be well to ask "What would be the point of human effort if popular alternative views of man were true?" All human behavior, we say, is at least in principle open to scientific explanation. And when we explain something scientifically we show how it "necessarily follows" from something else: we locate it in a causal sequence. One of the practical purposes of scientific explanation is that prediction of future events which will enable us to control them. If, we say, we could fully understand things or persons scientifically, we could, at least theoretically, fully predict their behavior. What, then, is the point of human effort, if all that men do is the necessary result of predictable causal factors of heredity and environment?

Many people who have asked this question have concluded that there really isn't any point: it's all a matter of genes, or glands, or subconscious forces, or economic factors, or political factors, or some other element in heredity or environment which is alleged to control all the rest. Indeed, the point of any scientific investigation of human affairs, whether in terms of natural or social science, is to show how and to what extent human affairs are determined by the forces in which a particular science specializes. Of course we realize that matters get more difficult as one deals with more complex behavior, and that the social sciences in particular always have to allow for the "independent variables" of human behavior. But these are at least in principle reducible to causal explanation.

Now the interesting thing is that lots of people who talk this way don't act as if they really believed that this is all there is to human behavior. Many of them are great exponents and defenders of human freedom. But how can men be free if all their actions are determined? Others seem to say that the behavior of all men except those in the know about the causes of behavior is determined. Thus the Marxist says that everybody else's theories are "mere ideologies"—tainted by those economic forces which only the Marxist really understands. But the proletariat are somehow magically exempt from ideological bias, because they have no class or imperialistic interests, by definition! Again, people with a superficial knowledge of psychology and psychoanalytic theory are likely to indulge in the smug pleasure of "psychologizing" everybody else's behavior, explaining just why Joe does this and Mary does that, while seeming oblivious to those psychological needs which seem to be determining their own behavior. Or an even stranger thing may happen: Our psychologizing friend may *delight* in acknowledging that he does all that he does because of childhood traumas or whatever, with the implication that he therefore really isn't responsible for his behavior. Yet he will balk at this line of reasoning when he wants to take credit for something he has done. Indeed, most of us seem to be determinists when it is to our advantage to be so, and proclaimers of freedom when our prestige is thereby enhanced. Obviously we are involved in contradictions here—of theory or practice or both.

Perhaps we should back up and ask just what we mean by "freedom." If we mean complete independence of causal factors, then clearly no human act is a free act. Anything we do is done in a context, and that context is open to causal explanation. Furthermore, if men really were free in the sense of being able to do anything they wanted to do at any moment, our whole educational enterprise would be pointless, and our moral scheme of responsibility, praise, and blame would be nonsensical. There would be no learning from experience, no development of character, no continuity of personal identity from one moment to the next. A man might choose to do one thing in one moment and a completely different thing in another. In a very real sense he would not be the same man in any two moments, and thus never responsible in one moment for his actions in another. A world which was completely free in the sense of being causally undetermined would be sheer chaos. Surely this is not what we mean by "freedom." Yet, on the other hand, if everything *is* causally determined, what's the point of effort? We are going to do what we are going to do anyway. "I can't help it," we say, "that's just the way I am."

Now let's focus a bit on that word "I." What do we mean when we say "that's the way *I* am," or "*I* had to do it because. . ."? From the standpoint of science, "I" am a complex of *instances* of universal laws. I am an instance of certain laws of heredity, and I am an example of upper-middle-class behavior in a suburban environment. To understand who I am is to know all the generalities of which I am an instance. In other words, I am not an irreducible *individual*; I am a *particular* instance of *universals*. Yet we realize that this is not quite the case, even from the standpoint of science. Even from this point of view it is true that I am I, and not somebody else. There is a sense in which I am unrepeatable and unique; the mold was broken when I was made. We may have to overlook this fact when we go about explaining ourselves in terms of our likeness to others, but the fact remains. We say we could predict everyone's behavior *if* we could fully know all the facts of their heredity and their environment—yet the fact is that no two people have exactly the same heredity and environment. Hereditary factors are differently arranged for each individual. (It is not clear whether the case of "identical twins" is an exception to the rule.) You are a part of my environment and I am a part of yours, so our environments differ in at least this important respect. Even from the standpoint of science, there is always a unique x in the environment-heredity equation for each human individual.

Maybe this is part of what we mean when we say that we are "free." My action is my action, and not somebody else's; therefore to that extent I, and I alone, am respon-

167

sible for it. Indeed, we say that people are irresponsible insofar as they are susceptible to the pressures of others, and that they are "real people" to the extent that they are uniquely and recognizably themselves in any situation. Their very knowledge of psychological and other factors in their make-up may give them the self-understanding necessary for "being themselves." They know what they're doing, we say, and their choices are *deliberate* because they are carefully *deliberated*.

But what and when is "choice"? Choice is that uniquely individual factor which intervenes between environmental or hereditary stimulus and behavioral response. And choice is always *now*. Only the present is the moment of choice. Once a choice is made, we can "look back on it" and "see" why we did what we did. But in the moment of choice we are not looking back, except insofar as past behavior, like the future goals toward which we look forward, is considered relevant to the choice itself. All deterministic theories of human behavior are in a sense retrospective. *"Given* situation *x,"* we say, "we can see why choice *y* was made." But there is always mystery in the *givenness* of "the given," and there may always be novelty in the present moment through which the future emerges. The mystery and the novelty are expressed and celebrated in the arts, just as the continuities and causal connections in behavior are investigated by the sciences. It is interesting to note that we call the arts "the *humanities*." These have to do with matters which are distinctively human. But insofar as it is man who is the scientist, science too is a humanistic enterprise—maybe the most human of all.

Now what has all this to do with the questions whether "everything is in the hands of God," and whether, if this were the case, there would be any point to human effort? What we have been suggesting is that we all hold that everything is in a sense "in the hands of" *something*. That is, there is some final context in terms of which we seek to understand human behavior. Some of us may say that everything is finally in the hands of economic forces; others may reply that, while economic forces are important, there is a sense in which we are in our own hands —or have ourselves *on* our hands! We are in some measure free to determine our own behavior. The self is an irreducible and enigmatic factor in the deterministic formula. We have the freedom of *self*-determination. The proper question is not whether we are determined or not, but rather by what (or whom?) we are determined. The sciences seek to enumerate causal forces, and the humanities articulate the mystery that is left out of the scientific accounts.

Is there, then, a word for the "total picture"? Men seem to need such a word, and they have used many. The favorite word of some of the Greeks was *moira*, "fate." After all was said about a human situation that could be said in terms of human motives and divine plans, they said, there remained the fact of "overarching fate," which ultimately controlled the affairs of gods and men alike. Men might to some extent know their fate, but their knowledge could not change their fate; indeed, the heroic attempts of some men to change their fate was the subject of ironic comment in Greek tragedy. Sometimes fate was portrayed in semi-human terms, but in the last analysis fate was viewed as inscrutable and impersonal: indifferent to the best-laid plans of gods and men. The portrayal of fate in Greek tragedy has a perennial appeal, and seems perennially relevant. It perhaps seems especially relevant today, because many of us would also say that in the last analysis we are creatures and subjects of impersonal and purposeless forces. Our very scientific enterprise is predicated on the proposition that this is the case. We can glory in the specifically human, even as its uniqueness is underscored by science itself; and we can do what we can to make the most of the situation in which we find ourselves—but the end of the matter may be, as T. S. Eliot put it, a whimper or a bang. We are, in the last analysis, fatalists. So what's the point of human effort?

"Well, at least," some say, "it's interesting to see how things turn out." The human drama is no less dramatic and no less intriguing, and heroism is no less heroic, for the fact that it's all finally a matter of fate. Indeed, struggle against fate is of the very essence of nobility. But notice how, when we talk this way, we keep slipping into personal terms for a matter we have declared to be impersonal. A fatalist keeps on talking as if fate *were* purposeful, though he doesn't know its (?) purposes. And in addition to all our talk about fate, there is talk about "fortune" and "luck." "Fortune smiles on us" or it (?) doesn't. "Lady Luck is with us" or *she* (!) isn't. "There's no need to worry, because nothing is going to happen until your number is up—and when it is, there's nothing you can do about it." "The only bullet to fear is the one that has your name on it—and you can't know which one that is." "Well, that's the way the ball bounces!" "Somebody," it seems, is "smiling" or "frowning"—but *capriciously*; "luck" is as gracious—or fickle—as a woman, begging the pardon of feminine readers. Somebody is calling the numbers or spinning the wheel, but nobody can know which number will be called or come up. Somebody is putting names on bullets, but that somebody is inscrutable.

Fate and Fortune were familiar words for the "total picture" in the world into which Christianity came—as familiar as they are now. Then, as now, Christians would not deny the reality of all those features of the world, and of man's understanding of it, which the words express. There *are* impersonal causal forces which men can partially understand, but which remain mysterious on the other side of understanding, and remain impersonal for all of man's humanizing. There are also events which strike us as capricious. But neither "mystery" nor "caprice" is the *last* word for the "total picture," Christians say. The last word is "providence." We are finally in the hands of neither impersonal fate nor capricious personality, but of that purposeful being whose nature was revealed in a Person, and whose partially understood mystery is communicated in the doctrine of the trinity. What we as persons have to do with *finally* is not impersonal. Human love is not a tragic aberration in a loveless world. It is a pale reflection of that love which, as Dante put it, "moves the stars"—and moved among men as a helpless babe in a manger and an agonized man on a cross. It is from this man, as seen in the total context we have sought to develop in this book, that the Christian gets his basic clue to the "total picture." He does not claim fully to understand that picture; indeed, the more he knows, the more he is aware of the finitude of his knowledge. But he knows enough to affirm—to bet his life, as it were, on the proposition—that the God revealed in Jesus Christ is the One with whom he has finally to do.

How does he "have to do" with that One? He has to

171

do as a person related to a Person, and not as thing related to the impersonal. This means that whatever control over the world the divine Personhood is said to exercise operates *through* and not at the *expense of* or *in spite of* human personality and human freedom. If what men have to do with finally were impersonal, then human freedom would be finally expendable. In spite of everything human, fate would have its way. Christians affirm that everything human is closest to, not farthest from, the One with whom humans have to do. Human freedom is of the essence of the *imago dei*. Divine providence undergirds and operates *through* human choice. Divine love seeks the response of human love, and a response which is not free is not a response of love. Thus the divine love respects the freedom of men to "go to Hell" *if they will*, rather than coerce them into Heaven. Indeed, Dante suggests that "Heaven" and "Hell" are simply the "states" of two human responses to the same divine love. (See also C. S. Lewis' *The Great Divorce*.) One is the "great negation"; the other, the great affirmation of freedom and its responsibilities. In the one, the denial of freedom renders community impossible, and its last images are of frozen impotence and futile rage. In the other, the affirmation of freedom makes possible the perfect community in which each is freely himself and each rejoices in the freely willed selfhood of others. Its last image is of the multifoliate rose, whose petals reflect with equal beauty the radiance of the Love at the center.

Yet sticky problems remain. *Do* Christians really say that God operates *through* human freedom? If so, what's all this business about "predestination"? Isn't it double-talk to say both that men are free and that everything happens because of the will of God? One can only suggest that in reflecting further on the last question one must take seriously, and work out the implications of, what has been suggested above with respect to the kind of relation Christians see between the divine will and human wills. The first question suggests further thought about the adequacy of the "pre" in the word "predestination." There is "destination," to be sure; Christians and non-Christians alike talk about "human destiny." The crucial issue is whether the "destination" of "destiny" is finally by personal or by impersonal forces; by capricious personality or by divine love. In any case the "pre" is an unfortunate prefix. It seems to point to God as one causal agent among others operating *in* the space-time continuum of "destiny." The words "before" and "after" apply literally only to the arrangement of events in space and time. But he in terms of whom these events as a whole are understood—or that which *expresses* one's basic posture *toward* the events "as a whole"—can be neither "before" nor "after." Recall that St. Augustine said the most appropriate time-word for relations to God is "now." In a sense this would be true of time-words for Fate and Fortune also. Yet with respect to the latter, as with respect to God, we talk as if they operated as agents among other agents in the before-and-after of time. Actually we cannot help talking that way, because human talk is time-talk. By stretching the imagination beyond any literal "sense," however, we may talk also of a source of space-time events which is "eternally now," or is "the eternal now": "in whom," using Biblical words, "there is no shadow of turning." We point toward that sense of "eternal now-ness" in lines like those of a familiar hymn: "A thousand ages in thy sight are like an evening gone. . ." Of course, incredibly swift passage of time is still passage of *time*; but the image may evoke a sense of that which is, with respect to all befores and afters of time, simply and fully *now*. The point is that when Christians have spoken of "pre-destination" they might just as well have spoken of "post-destination," or even better of simple "destination." "*Now*," says the Christian, "human personality is responsible to divine love—whenever 'now' may be."

At times Christian theologians like Augustine, and especially John Calvin, have been so concerned to keep steadily before the Christian the priority of the divine sovereignty—to remind men that they are not God, and that the universe does not finally revolve around them— that they have seemed to exalt the divine sovereignty at the expense of human freedom. Others, like Augustine's opponent Pelagius, have been so concerned to affirm that it is human freedom *through* which sovereign divine love operates that they have seemed to diminish the sovereignty of the divine. Christians have at times acted as if there were nothing for "men of God" to do but sit down. Others have acted as if they were dead-sure about what God was up to in a given situation, and sure of just what they had to do in order for the divine purpose to be realized. Many have gone so far as to indicate that the divine purpose awaited their decision, and many so-called prayers seem to be full of advice to deity as to how the world should be run. The Christian church has its share of moral cowards, and of bigots, and of moral illiterates. But the Christian belief that "everything is in the hands of God" has also provided many with what seems to them to be the most logical basis for meaningful human effort. Awareness of the divine sovereignty has produced humility. Awareness of human freedom under-

girded by that which is foundational in reality has produced the courage to defy tyranny in high places of state
and church. Humble courage, or courageous humility,
has characterized the lives of multitudes who have believed that there *is* "point to human effort" *because*
"everything is in the hands of God."

*"Christianity might make some sense as a private philosophy
of life . . ."*

Is Christianity a philosophy of life? This is a question
on which we must reflect further. But first let us ask
whether Christianity is merely a private affair of any
kind. It is true that it deals with men's most intimate as
well as with their ultimate concerns. In the last analysis
no one else can do our living for us—and certainly we
die alone. In most of this book we have dealt mainly with
some basic Christian affirmations as they relate to the
individual's understanding of fundamental issues of life
and death. Yet a moment's reflection should recall that
from the beginning Christianity has always seen the individual in a social setting. A basic assumption of the
faith is that men are bound together in the context of
creation. "No man," says the Christian poet, "is an island
. . ." If the first and greatest commandment of Biblical
faith is that one shall love God with all his being, the
second is implied by the first: one shall love his neighbor as himself. "All the rest is commentary", said Rabbi
Hillel; "on these two commandments hang all of the law
and the prophets," said Jesus of Nazareth.

Certainly the faith of Israel is an irreducibly communal faith. In the Bible it is a *people* who are called to
do God's work in the world, and their work is to be a
blessing to all peoples. The divine purpose is to fulfill

175

the just aspirations of all people in a New Society, in a New Age. Christianity, we have seen, was born in the conviction that the New Age and the New Society were at hand. Jesus spoke always of the Kingdom of God as a social fact—never as a merely individual fulfillment. In all his teaching the nature and quality of the individual's life before God is reflected in his relations with other men. The earliest Christians defined themselves as members of the *community* of the New Covenant. A continuing task of Christians through the centuries has been to determine the nature of that community, and to define its relation to other communities to which Christians belong, such as those of family, and state. To trace the process by which they have done this, and the various definitions at which they have arrived, would require another volume at least as long as this one. The reader is urged to look at some good ones already in existence which do just this.

Meanwhile, we may in brief summary recall that Jesus did not see membership in and loyalty to the Kingdom of God as negating a due and proper respect for and participation in the affairs of the state. When he was asked whether it was lawful to pay tribute to Caesar he asked some one to show him a coin. The fact that a coin was produced, in part answered the question: without government there would be no commerce, no coins. "Render, then, unto Caesar that which is Caesar's," he said. But the state does not claim final or exclusive allegiance; there are things that do not belong to Caesar. While recognizing the good of the state, men must "render unto God that which is God's."

Nevertheless, Jesus was executed by the state on charges of treason; he claimed, it was said, a kingship that was Caesar's alone. After his death the Christian community was tolerated by the state except when it seemed to disturb the peace; its leaders recognized the state as a part of God's good creation, which provided that order which made possible the spread of the gospel. Perhaps it was about to be supplanted by the New Order of God's Kingdom, but meanwhile good Christians should be good citizens. Of course the state was not willing to let it go at that. In periods when the state was under attack from without and from within, it took a dim view of those Christian citizens who recognized a loyalty higher than the loyalty to Caesar— who even refused to burn a pinch of incense before Caesar's image. Waves of persecution resulted, until, in the fourth century, the persecuted faith was made the official religion of the empire.

This state of affairs presented the church with grave moral and social problems, as well as with the doctrinal problems we have previously noted. How could the church serve as the conscience and critic of the state when the state supported the church? Men were to agonize over this question for centuries to come. But the immediate response was a great vision of Christendom: an undivided society built on Christian principles, of which the state would be one arm and the church the other. The job of the church, said St. Augustine in his *City of God,* is to be the earthly reflection of that perfect society of peace based on ordered love, which is the goal of all human striving. The church as an institution, like the state, will inevitably contain all sorts and conditions of men; but the church's vision of the "Heavenly City" might serve as a flying goal of all social development until vision and reality became one, in God's time.

In succeeding centuries there were those who felt that the City of Man was too corrupt for men to live the Christian life in its normal structures and channels. So they withdrew, first to hermit, and then to communal, monastic existence. Their aim from the beginning was not simply to escape from the world in order to save their individual souls. In the very practice of Christian devotion, solitary or in company with others, they would be praying for others. Soon their work for society became broader than the essential work of prayer. St. Benedict of Nursia organized a community which placed equal emphasis on prayer, study, and manual labor. Here was something new under the sun—the idea that menial labor, reserved in pagan societies for second-class citizens, could be an appropriate means of praising God. And the study and teaching of the Benedictines and others helped preserve the intellectual life of man in the chaotic centuries of early European civilization. The care of the sick also was recognized to be a necessary part of the Christian way of life, and some monastic orders made that their special concern. When new times demanded new expressions of Christian social responsibility, St. Francis of Assisi could take the gospel and works of mercy to the highways and to the street corners of the new commercial cities, and St. Dominic and others could found orders that would have a special concern for the new university life of Europe.

Then in the sixteenth century Protestant Reformers concluded that nothing less than "monasticizing the laity" was an adequate expression of the gospel in society. Luther said that a scullery maid on her knees to scrub was as truly praising God as a monk on his knees to pray, if both were there with the intention of praising God. Luther felt that Christian charity begins at home, and he was not too sanguine about the direct relevance of Gospel counsels of love to more complex societies beyond the home and the neighborhood. The state is an order of creation which has to take account of the fact that not all citizens in the state are Christians, and not all Christians practice what they preach. But there are lines beyond which the state can not go; the church must be free to preach the gospel and administer the sacraments according to the will of God. John Calvin, on the other hand, was convinced that a practicing Christian must strive for a Christian commonwealth. Not only private life, but also corporate political and economic life, must be conformed to the will of God as revealed in scripture. Calvin's Geneva would have a universal system of free education, a democratically structured organization of state and church, a proper sense of Christian discipline in daily life—and there would be no poor in Geneva. Calvin's ideals were to work as a social ferment in Britain and in the New World, as well as on the European continent.

Yet Calvin and Luther, as well as many of their English reforming colleagues, still maintained the corporate ideal of an undivided Christendom, with church and state equally responsible for its realization. Alongside them grew up men and movements convinced that the church could be a faithful witness to the Kingdom of God only if it were separate from the state. When the American experiment got under way in the New World a variety of social and political circumstances combined to make this view the official one for the churches in the

United States. Just what it means for concrete issues of public policy is a constant problem for church and state.

Certainly it does not mean that churchmen have no special obligations as citizens. In our times as in New Testament days, acceptance of the Christian way of life is understood by Christians to be also acceptance of special responsibilities for the welfare of others, whether this responsibility be expressed in intimate and personal ways or less directly through forms of economic and political action. Most Christians are agreed that no specific form of social or political organization can be equated with the Kingdom of God. Indeed, most are convinced that loyalty to the Kingdom entails continuous critique and transformation of existing social structures. There is disagreement with respect to the direction of change in given circumstances, and with respect to the most "Christian" techniques to be used in the achievement of change. Some Christians feel that others betray the faith in making too easy compromises with dubious means in order to gain ambiguously Christian ends. Others feel that some of their fellow Christians are so lofty in their ideals and so squeamish about the techniques they will employ to reach them that their social witness becomes ineffective, or inadvertently aids the forces of evil against which they would fight. But beneath all the divergence of opinion about church and state, and about ways and means of social action, there is an unbroken continuity of conviction among Christians that, whatever else Christianity may be, it is not merely a *private* affair. In all Christian visions of the fulfillment of human life it is a perfect community in perfect communion with the divine, rather than individual beatification or absorption, which expresses the substance of Christian hope.

And now let us ask whether the agency of that hope is a "philosophy of life". If this term is meant to include the pattern of all of one's hopes and fears as well as his principles; all of the texture of his relations to others as well as his private theory of the world—or his theory of his private world; all of his doubts as well as his beliefs, and all of his affirmations as well as his criticism; if it is to include that which he *worships* as well as that which he knows or believes—then perhaps Christianity could be called a philosophy of life. But clarity would seem to demand that the term "philosophy" be somewhat more definite, and more restricted, than this. Of course a favorite occupation of philosophers is debating what philosophy is (and in a sense it might be said that philosophy *is* "debating what philosophy is"). But one or two general kinds of human concern have been traditionally associated with the term "philosophy."

One of these is a concern for synoptic vision. In addition to the lineaments of life and the world disclosed by specialized forms of inquiry, philosophers have sought to discover the perennial traits of whatever is, and to see how the view of one human discipline relates to the views of others in a synoptic whole. They have been concerned for meta-physics, that which comes after physics or any other scientific inquiry, and for the relation of scientific to moral and esthetic constructions of experience. The search is for depth and for perspective. We communicate something of this sense of philosophy when we say of a person who is grappling with a difficult experience, "He's taking it philosophically": that is, he is taking it with some sense of its relation to a broader scheme of things—with a sense of perspective.

Another concern of philosophy is with criticism and analysis. It has been said that the distinguishing characteristic of the philosophic enterprise is that it leaves no assumptions unexamined. The philosopher wants to know how the scientist does what he does, and what he must take for granted to do it; he engages in a critique of scientific inquiry. And he is equally interested in critiques of all other forms of inquiry and enjoyment open to men. He is the taker-apart of opinions and habits, the interrogator of cherished beliefs, the analyst of talk and of conduct. He is, said Socrates, the gadfly of society. He may not answer many questions, but he may help men to see what their questions really are—to sort out kinds of questions and kinds of answers, and thereby clarify discourse. Many philosophers today would say that this is the primary if not the sole job of philosophy, and they look askance at the more ambitious speculations of those who are still concerned with synoptic vision. The proper job of philosophy is question-*asking*, not question-*answering*, they say.

Those who conceive of philosophy as vision would agree that they are not out to answer questions in the same sense or in the same way a scientist is. Affirmations about the generic traits of being cannot be verified in a laboratory. Yet the philosopher is obliged to make his vision as rational and as responsible as possible. His theory must begin and end in gross fact, and he must depart no farther from fact that rigorous logic will permit. If this concern for what can be proved, at least in a recognizably rational extension of the term "proof," rules out of his vision many of the hopes and objects of religious faith, then so much the worse for religious faith. It is better, a philosopher might say, to live without the comforts of the unprovable; to face life squarely and to face it whole, with courage and with rationality. The philosophic way is not the easy way, and most philosophers are aware of the fact that not many men will choose it. But "all things excellent," said Spinoza, "are as difficult as they are rare."

Shall we, then, call Christianity a "philosophy of life"? St. Paul was convinced that it is "a more excellent way". The way of which he spoke, the way of Christian love, is not unaware of the need to know—or of the limitations of our knowledge: "now we know in part". And it is not a way which shuts its eyes to the ugly and the irrational: it "endures all things." It knows of and extols heroism and magnanimity—"bodies given to be burned" and goods given to the poor. But all of this, without love, said Paul, "profits nothing"—adds up to an uncertain, or a negative, result. To all that may be *known*, religion adds that which may be *believed*. The faith that undergirds and supplements knowledge is not, in the Christian view, contrary to knowledge, or irrational. But it adds the substance of hope to the structure of the actual. It is willing to accept "the evidence of things not seen." Yet the acceptance is not a "blind" acceptance. It is rather because eyes have been opened to a personal and sustaining reality that they need not be shut to the chaos and absurdity of life in the foreground of vision.

Christianity, then, is a *way*—not primarily a way of knowing, or of behaving, or even of believing—but a way of *living*, in all the dimensions of life. This is to say that it is a way of worship. Man's worship, we have said, is his expression of his primary relations to that which—or to

Him Who—is believed to be worthy of complete devotion. Beyond the goods worthy of qualified devotion is the One who is to be loved with all one's being. Beyond the limited concerns for relative goods is the unconditional concern for the ultimate good. Christianity proclaims good news about the ultimate good. Its message is intended for, and its fellowship is designed to include, men and women of all ages, degrees of intelligence and sensibility, races and nations, places and times. It is concerned for the totality of their lives. Thus it appreciates and should nurture the concerns of scientists and philosophers, as well as of poets and prelates, and of hewers of wood and drawers of water. But it is more than a philosophy of life, just as it is more than a private affair. It is, in brief, a religious faith.

". . . but who could ever think he had life all figured out?"

Who, indeed? Certainly no one who is a Christian in fact and in faith rather than in fiction, if our brief study of Christianity is anywhere near the mark in distinguishing between fact, faith, and fiction. To the extent that Christians have ever given the impression that they have life all figured out they have departed from the spirit of humility and openness which has characterised the lives of the saints through the ages. The Founder of the Faith sweat drops of blood in Gethsemane and uttered a cry of God-forsakenness from his cross, even as he died in final confidence. St. Paul knew the agony of doubt and of moral frustration as well as he knew the whip of persecution and the perils of shipwreck. He also knew that "we hold these treasures in earthen vessels." St. Augustine knew all the pangs of intellectual despair and psycho-

logical conflict before he knew the joy of Christian peace
—and that peace was the context of continued intellectual struggle in understanding and articulating the faith.
St. Thomas deposited his monumental work of theological and philosophical synthesis on the altar as an unworthy sacrifice. Learned doctors and unlettered servants
of the church alike have known that *their* truth was not
the truth, and that for the vital Christian the process of
free and open inquiry never ends. There are always, they
have said, more riches to be found in "the unsearchable
riches of Christ."

Beyond that, there is always the possibility that the
Christian may be wrong about the whole business. He
espouses a faith, not a certainty. If he can maintain his
faith only by ignoring or suppressing disturbing thoughts
and threatening experiences, something is wrong with
his faith. He will spend so much time trying to "save" it
that it obviously could not be saving him. The life of the
Christian is completely open and honest, in continuous
dialogue with experience as it comes, and with opposing
views of life, or it has lost contact with its sources. Fear
of not being able to "handle" a question about life or an
experience of life is a measure of unbelief or false belief.
Unwillingness to admit that one does not have the answers reflects the anxious need for self-justification which
the good news is said to overcome. The questions with
which we have dealt in this book are, we believe, honest
questions sincerely posed by many honest people in our
day. Asking them and others like them is the necessary
first step toward that clarification which alone can make
either an affirmation or a denial of the faith intelligently
responsible. There is an obvious presumption in the
answers which we have offered. Who is to say what *the*

Christian faith is, or what *the* Christian will do about this or that, as we have said? Who can know finally how honest the answers are? In the language of a Christian prayer, only One "unto whom all hearts are open, all desires known, and from whom no secrets are hid." If either the reader or the author stops asking and answering questions as faithfully and as honestly as he can when he closes the pages of this book, the book will not have accomplished its purpose. Some readers will decide that if *this* is the fact and fiction of the Christian faith, then for them Christianity is obsolete. Others may find that a judgment of obsolescence is at least premature, and that Christianity may be, after all, of more than sentimental or historical interest.